UNION JOB RELATIONS

10-Hour Sessions Outline
and
Reference Material

UNION JOB RELATIONS

A TRAINING WITHIN INDUSTRY PROGRAM

The Union Job Relations program is a special adaptation of the Job Relations program, which was prepared in order to give union stewards basic instruction in the skill of leadership.

WAR MANPOWER COMMISSION
Bureau of Training
Training Within Industry Service
1944

Originally published as *Union Job Relations: Sessions Outline and Reference Material*, released in 1944 by the War Manpower Commission of the Bureau of Training, Washington, District of Columbia.

Enna Products
1602 Carolina St.
Suite B3
Bellingham, WA 98229
Telephone: (360) 306-5369
Fax: (905) 481-0756
E-mail: info@enna.com

Cover Design/Illustrations by Khemanand Shiwram
Editor: Collin McLoughlin
Associate Editor: Shawna Gilleland

Library of Congress Control Number: 2009938941

Library of Congress Cataloging-in-Publication Data

United States. Bureau of Training. War Manpower Commission. 1944
        Union Job Relations: 10-Hour Sessions Outline and Reference Material

        ISBN 978-1-897363-95-9
        1. Training Within Industry   2. Training of employees 3. Organizational change
4. Productivity–Increasing through training   I. Title

Dedicated to the men and women of The Greatest Generation.

July 1944.

To The War Production Trainer:

Your Union Job Relations sessions can have for your union and for the war production effort a constructive influence, perhaps never before experienced. You have an unusual <u>opportunity</u> of influencing stewards to improve their everyday relationships on the job.

Representing workers' alone is not enough. Stewards must give every man and woman they represent the leadership that enlists cooperation and teamwork. You can help stewards to get this skill of working with people—it is your <u>obligation</u> to stress its importance to them.

You should strive with all the energy and diligence you possess to lead each Union Job Relations group in the very best way possible—and to do a <u>better</u> job with each succeeding group.

To assure a uniformly high standard, work from this outline <u>always</u>. Do not deviate from it. Do not trust to your memory, regardless of the number of sessions you put on.

Once again, leadership in Union Job Relations presents an <u>opportunity</u> and an <u>obligation</u>.

Sincerely,

C. R. Dooley

C. R. Dooley, Director,

Training Within Industry Service.

SUMMARY OF PURPOSE AND EMPHASIS OF UNION JOB RELATIONS SESSIONS

I To establish the fact that everyday job relationships are one of the most important parts of the war production steward's job.
To present the foundations for good relations.
To establish a 4-step method for meeting job relations situations.

A steward gets results through people. People must be treated as individuals. Good stewardship prevents many problems, but the steward must know how to handle those that do arise.

II To develop skill in Step 1, "Get the Facts."
To give the group practice on Step 1 through emphasis on this step in a problem presented by the Trainer, and to give members of the group practice in looking at the 4-step method in two problems brought in by stewards.

Complete facts must be known or obtained. Opinions and feelings must be found out and considered along with facts. It is necessary to look at an individual because people are not alike.

III To develop skill in Step 2, "Weigh and Decide."
To give the group practice on Step 2 through emphasis on this step in a problem presented by the Trainer and to give members of the group practice in three problems brought in by stewards.

Decisions are made on the basis of facts properly evaluated and related.

IV To establish the importance of Steps 3 and 4, "Take Action" and "Check Resutls."
To give the group practice in Steps 3 and 4 through emphasis on these steps in a problem presented by the Trainer and to give members of the group practice in looking at the 4-step method in three problems brought in by stewards.

The steward must know his responsibility. He must watch the timing of his action and follow-up, and watch for effect on the objective, on the individual, on the group, on production, and on union standing.

V To give members of the group practice in looking at the 4-step method in two problems brought in by stewards.
To review and summarize foundations, 4-step method, and tips for getting opinions and feelings.
To consider the other working relationships of the steward—to other union officials and to plant supervisors.

Further develop the habit of using the complete method. Point out application of the method to steward's other relationships. A steward gets results through people.

CONTENTS

Strategy for Union Job Relations

Training Within Industry looks at the training of stewards as a five-part job. That is, the steward has five needs.

1. Knowledge of the Work
2. Knowledge of Responsibilities
3. Skill in Instructing
4. Skill in Improving Methods
5. Skill in Leading

Union Job Relations is a streamlined, intensive program designed to give union stewards practice in developing Skill in Leading. It is not intended to provide any training in the "Knowledge of Responsibilities" area—the job of training stewards in the policies, agreements, and regulations of a particular union must be done by the union.

Union Job Relations aims to develop a skill—not to give stock answers on grievances, or to provide industrial relations background on such subjects as rates of pay, safety, or working conditions.

Since Union Job Relations is focused on working with people, descriptions of what happens to people are the materials for this program. In the standard Sessions Outlines there are four of these problems, each of which is used at the specific point for a particular reason. The time of the members of the group is spent mostly on the handling of their own problems which they bring in for group discussion.

Union Job Relations is limited to groups of ten stewards. Experience has shown that this number is desirable. A smaller group does not provide enough variety of problems and a larger group provides too much material for inclusion within the ten hours.

In some instances observers have been admitted to the sessions with the purpose of giving them familiarity with the contents of the program as it normally operates. These observers are requested to stay in character as observers and are not permitted to join in the discussion. When there are observers present it should be made clear to them in advance that they are not being asked to attend in order to assist in lining up how the program should operate—this is a standardized program and no deviations or changes are to be made.

Training Within Industry urges the use of this program for all of the union's stewards and grievance committee members. Those who are new on the job of representing other people need help and training more than those who have had experience on the job.

However, if the union says that all its officers would benefit by this way of looking at union relationships or that the pressure of present production conditions has brought about an increase in the problems which a steward must handle, the same training program will apply to persons who have been on higher level jobs for some time. The nature of the problems brought in and the discussion may be quite different from those in a group of new shop stewards.

If in such a group, their problems tend to be unanimously well handled and the Trainer should make a specific appeal for the bringing in of situations which have had poor results, and also for the kind which may be sized up in advance to get good results through preventive action.

Out of the experience of preparing this program good reasons have developed for doing what is done, in the way it is done, and at a particular time.

SESSION I—PRESENTATION OF FOUNDATIONS FOR GOOD RELATIONS AND THE 4-STEP METHOD

Getting Acquainted

Ask each man in the group about his own background and present union responsibilities. This brings quick and easy participation from every member of the group. The members are being asked to tell something about which they and only they have the story. Also, the Trainer gains valuable information about the people with whom he will be working for the next ten hours.

The Steward's Five Needs

The five needs are discussed to emphasize to stewards that, regardless of their industry or department, they must be well versed in two knowledges and three skills in order to be effective stewards. The Skill of Leading is covered in these sessions.

Chart on Steward's Responsibility

The development of the chart with "people" in the center and the arrow linking the steward to the people is a quick means of focusing attention on the subject-matter of Union Job Relations. There is also real group participation in the development of this chart, as members point out their responsibilities.

Foundations for Good Relations

There are certain basic points which are followed by effective stewards. While Union Job Relations does not give a great deal of time in the ten hours to these foundations as such, nevertheless it is necessary to recognize their importance and to put them across in a way which will gain acceptance. They form the underlying spirit of good relationships and promote good stewardship.

Chart on the Individual

The pulling out of one person from the group of people, through whom the steward gets results, is done because of the need of pointing out that people must be treated as individuals since they are different in background, interests, and tastes.

The Mike Problem

This problem is told by the Trainer. It is short and the telling gives it much more reality than reading. Also, the members of the group will be telling their problems later, and the Trainer should set the pattern he wishes used.

This situation was handled in a way that got poor results. Such a problem was chosen for several reasons. First, it will often be necessary for the group to be critical about the results which a steward gets when he does not use the complete 4-step method. It is easier to start this pattern presenting a problem which does not personally concern any member of the group.

Second, the problem is a very simple one from which it is easy to pull out the positive points which need to be made. Asking where the steward skidded almost invariably sets up the main points of Job Relations' 4-step method.

The telling of the problem is broken into two parts in order to get emphasis for the importance of starting the 4-step pattern at the beginning—getting facts before attempting to make a decision and take action. The discussion begins in the pattern which will be followed throughout. That is, it is necessary to first pull out just what the steward is trying to accomplish. This pattern of discussion enables the leader to keep away from the criticism of decisions by focusing on the use of the method. The four main steps on the card are pulled out from the Mike problem. Experience has shown that the discussion is belabored if the attempt is made to also develop the sub-points.

How Problems Arise

This material is presented in order to show stewards that they often can get in on situations early; that an advance size-up may prevent problems. This also will suggest to members of the group other problems which they might bring into the discussion.

Problem Sheets

The problem sheets are used to get conviction from the group that the Union Job Relations program is aimed at the kinds of problems that stewards encounter every day. It also gives hints on the type of problems which the members of the group will bring in for discussion.

Requests for Problems

Members of the group prefer to talk about their own problems rather than those brought in by the Trainer. The four standard problems are used because it is necessary to insure that certain points of the method are put across. But, once these points are worked in, the rest of the time is given to the problems which the men themselves are living with every day. The problems are restricted to those which are within the steward's own job to handle, something he can and must do something about.

SESSION II—IMPORTANCE OF GETTING THE FACTS

The Tom Problem

This problem is chosen to show the necessity of getting the facts and the importance of remembering that opinions and feelings must be considered the same as facts. The problem also gives some hints as to the way in which you get personal facts.

This problem is read, as exact words are important. Since it must be well read, which involves previous practice, it is specified that the Trainer read both parts of the dialogue.

This particular problem points to the difference between facts about the man and facts about the machine—both are necessary in order to have the whole story. The members of the group are also given a hint that it is sometimes necessary to probe a bit for the meaning behind words.

This problem points out the special importance of handling confidential material properly.

At a number of places the Trainer stops reading in order that the group may discuss specific points. It is possible in this way to get recognition of a few of the tips for getting personal opinions and feelings, which will later be developed and summarized.

Problems Brought in by Stewards

In the first steward's problem, and all succeeding ones, the man who is to present a problem should come to the head of the table with the Trainer. It has been found that shifting of position in the room is welcome and there appears to be a certain advantage in focusing on the man in this particular way. In the handling of the steward's problem the objective is pulled out to open the discussion. The Trainer must at all times be careful to key the comments, to "Did he follow the 4 steps?"—not to "Did he make a good decision?" The discussion must be handled so that the steward who presents the problem gets practice in using the 4 steps (see Standard Procedure, Reference Section).

Request to Consider Several Problems

Since occasionally a group member who is new or reluctant to talk does not wish to bring a problem for discussion, and also because some problems are so simple that any lengthy discussion would be belabored, it is sometimes necessary to have more than one problem from some members.

If a man says that he does not have any problems in his department, review the problem sheet again and ask such questions as "Does anyone ever think he's not getting a square deal?" "Did anyone ever complain about not getting a raise?" "Are any changes coming?" etc. If the man is obviously unwilling to present a problem after spending some time on reconsidering kinds of problems, do not press him too far. This would be poor Job Relations. (He cannot, however, be certified if he does not present a problem.)

Request for Problems with Poor Results

If all problems are well handled, discussion is not as interesting as if a diagnostic technique can be used to show where the steward skidded.

SESSION III—BASIS FOR DECISIONS

The session is opened by showing that a doctor, in getting the symptoms of a patient, goes through a process quite like the Job Relations 4-step method. Comparison with the doctor is used to show that the 4-step method has universal application, that it is specifically followed in a prominent profession, and perhaps, most important of all, to show that the doctor needs and gets much confidential information which he must handle well or it will not again be available to him.

The Old Hand Problem

This situation, which ended in poor results, is used to stress Step 2, "Weigh and Decide." It brings out the necessity of using all the facts and weighing them before making a final decision. The poor decision was reached because the steward first did not properly evaluate the facts which he had, and second, because he did not have the whole story.

SESSION IV—CHECKING RESULTS OF PREVENTIVE ACTION

The problem of the first Woman Supervisor is used as an example of good results of preventive action. The problem involves a number of people, and the subject is one which is current in many war production plants. The members of the group are also given a tip to work through those people who are recognized as natural, but informal, leaders.

Effect of Change

This subject is brought up to show that the problem of the first Woman Supervisor is not a "Woman" problem, but one typifying "change." Change is usually resented, and stewards need to take preventive action.

SESSION V—A STEWARD'S OTHER WORK RELATIONSHIPS

Request for Statements on Use of Job Relations

By getting the members themselves to pull out the advantages to them, personally, of following a method which will improve the quality of decisions and actions and which also shows the importance of checking results, the selling of Job Relations is completed.

Chart

The steward's responsibility chart, as used in Session I, is now amplified in order to point out to the steward the important position which he is in and to give recognition to it. This chart also offers the opportunity of again stressing "Get the Facts." The Trainer develops the idea that getting the facts will be useful in any relationship that the steward has, and that in a number of cases he will be responsible for giving the facts.

Closing Statement

The members of the group must leave with the feeling that what they do does matter, that it is very important. When the Trainer has made this point the session should be ended no matter what time it is. After a high point has once been reached, the whole effect can be ruined by keeping the members straining at a discussion in order to fill the hours.

INTRODUCTION OF UNION JOB RELATIONS TRAINER BY MANAGEMENT REPRESENTATIVE

(Trainer to provide union representative with copy of this page)

Union Job Relations is:

    a streamlined program for war industry from Training Within Industry

    developed by TWI and union leaders from industrial experience

    parallel to a supervisory Job Relations program.

The union officers:

    have approved this program

    want it for this union

    expect you to attend each session, and be here on time.

This is *your* meeting —

    no reports are going to be made to the union, except on attendance.

There will be:

    5 two-hour meetings

    held at _____ in _____ room, on _____

This program is important:

    the union expects you to do a good job—includes good relations with the people you represent

    the union knows you are going to get some real help

    this method will show you how to be a more effective steward.

This is Mr. _____

UNION JOB RELATIONS TRAINER'S INTRODUCTION WHEN NO MANAGEMENT REPRESENTATIVE ATTENDS

I am _____

The union officers:

    have approved the Job Relations Program

    want it for this union.

Job Relations is:

    a streamlined program for war industry from Training Within Industry

    developed by TWI and union leaders from industrial experiece

    parallel to a supervisory Job Relations program.

This is *our* meeting —

    no reports will be made to the union, except on attendance.

There will be:

    5 two-hour meetings

    held at _____ in _____ room, on _____

CODE

CAPITALS . . . . Section Heads

Horizontal line across page . . . . Encloses section for timing

Plain type . . . . Trainer says in own words

★ Star in front of line . . . . Trainer says verbatim

Material between lines . . . . Board Work

Bracket . . . . Instruction to trainer

PRESENTATION OF FOUNDATIONS FOR GOOD RELATIONS AND 4-STEP METHOD

Time Table

Allow 5 min

INTRODUCTION BY UNION OFFICER

(recommended procedure)

Give union officer copy of outline (page xviii).
Best results are obtained when a union officer opens the session.

5 min to here

Introduction by trainer (emergency only). Use outline (page xix) when impossible to get union officer to open the session.

Allow 10 min

GETTING ACQUAINTED

1. Tell your own background of union experience. This is important even if you know all members of the group.

2. Have stewards introduce themselves.

   Use name cards.

   Ask each man to tell you:

   work—department—number under jurisdiction — union experience.

3. If there are observers, explain:

   They wish to know more about the program.

   They do not enter the discussion, ask questions, or make remarks.

4. Stress—our meeting—problems discussed here are confidential—no names—give reasons— get agreement.

5. Those who attend all five sessions and present a problem will receive certificates.

15 min to here

DISCUSS THE STEWARD'S FIVE NEEDS

In these meetings we are going to use the term "steward" a great deal.

★ For the purpose of our discussions, when we refer to the
★ steward, we mean any member of the union elected or
★ appointed to represent other members..

★ You are all stewards.

Good stewards realize that they have five needs.

Let's take a look at these needs. They are:

★ 1. Knowledge of the Work

★ 2. Knowledge of Responsibilities

★ 3. Skill in Instructing

★ 4. Skill of Improving Methods

★ 5. Skill in Leading

1. *Knowledge of the Work* refers to the information which makes your job different from all other jobs.

A steward, to properly represent his constituents, should have a knowledge of their work in order to represent them in matters concerning production, safety, rates, and job classification. He needs to know:

materials	tools	operations
machines	processes	

2. *Knowledge of Responsibilities* refers to the particular union and company situations regarding:

Contract between union and management	National Labor Relations Act
Workmen's compensation	Union constitution and bylaws
Unemployment insurance	Policies of the War Labor Board
Policies and practices of the local union	Plant policies and practice
Relationships between department and plants	Safety Rules
	Schedules

These are different in every union and in every company. Hence this knowledge of responsibilities must be supplied locally.

2

Every steward, to do his job, must have a clear understanding of his authority and responsibilities as a part of his local union. He must also know the company's own rules and policies.

These local responsibilities are the "ground rules" under which every steward has to work.

3. *Skill in Instructing* is needed so that the steward can instruct other union members in the ways of doing union work. It is important for every union to give its stewards help in this field.

4. *Skill of Improving Methods* helps the steward to make specific and workable suggestions for new production techniques which will make the job easier and safer for his people. This skill is also needed in order to improve methods of doing union work.

5. *Skill in Leading* helps the steward to improve his ability in working with his people. There are basic principles that, when applied day in and day out, will tend to keep relations smooth and prevent problems from arising.

By pointing out the ways that problems do arise one can readily see that preventive action can be taken.

This applies particularly in anticipating changes that may not be readily accepted and in sensing changes in output, attitudes, and relationships.

However, when problems do arise, there is an organized procedure to handle such problems that helps get better results from the action we take.

STRESS THE FACT THAT SKILLS ARE ACQUIRED BY PRACTICE

The steward is not born with this skill. He must acquire it by actual practice. Just as soon as this skill is acquired by a steward he becomes more effective in the doing of his job. In these five 2-hour sessions, we will discuss this Skill in Leading which we shall call Union Job Relations.

DESCRIBE STEWARD'S PROBLEMS AS REGARDS JOB RELATIONS

1. Too few people realize that the steward's job is complex and difficult.

Unions want better relations among their own members and with management. The union wants better handling of complaints and better handling of real grievances.

3

This always requires the loyalty and cooperation of the members of the union.

Can we do something which will improve loyalty and cooperation? That is the purpose of these meetings.

When a machine is installed in a department, a handbook comes with it—or there may be a mechanic specially qualified in how that particular piece of machinery works, and directions on how to keep it in good operating condition, or what to do when it breaks down.

Stewards get new people all the time, but handbooks don't come with them.

How are you going to make those new members good union men? What will you do if they fail?

A union member tends to judge the whole union in terms of the treatment he receives from his own steward.

Remember when you joined the union—the first contact you had with your steward? I still remember.
(Illustrate)

There are thousands of people on union committee jobs today who were only members a short time ago.

As time goes, on thousands more men and women will have to become stewards or assume committee jobs.

Some of these people—some men, some women—have long backgrounds as members, some do not.

These new stewards and committeemen must quickly learn to work through people.

They must recognize that they can get their jobs done only through the cooperation of the members whom they represent.

Stewards, new and old alike, are confronted with the problem of obtaining the cooperation of:

- people who have never worked before
- people who have had steady work but of a different nature
- people who have never been members of a union
- people who present complaints and grievances which can't be processed

Newly elected stewards also my have the problem of obtaining the cooperation of people who:

- know more about the union than they do
- have many more years of service within the union than they have
- have served as stewards or lost in an election for stewards

4

Try to get agreement.

All stewards have to understand the attitudes of higher union stewards and secure their cooperation.

To meet such problems some kind of training in the special skill of leading is necessary.

This skill of working with people has long been recognized as a mark of good stewardship.

2. What do we mean by "good stewardship"?

★ Good stewardship is looking after the interests of the
★ people you represent.

★ 3. Now, in these sessions I'm not going to tell you how to
★ run your job.

But experienced stewards have developed a skill in working with people.

This skill can be learned.

It saves stewards a lot of headaches.

Good stewards need and develop skill in working with people.

35 min
to here

Let's see what we can find out about this skill.

Allow
10 min

SHOW THAT A STEWARD MEETS HIS RESPONSIBILITIES THROUGH RELATIONSHIPS WITH PEOPLE

★ 1. What are the common titles for different levels of
★ union officers?

These may be suggested:

district comitteeman	international representative
steward	president of the local
chief steward	member of executive board

For the purpose of our discussion, when we refer to a "steward" we mean ANYBODY WHO REPRESENTS PEOPLE OR WHO IS ELECTED OR APPOINTED TO A SPECIFIC UNION JOB.

Write "Steward" and enclose in a box near top of left third of board.

Steward

5

★ This steward not only represents people, he gets results
★ through people. The steward gets his work done, not
★ through authority, but through leadership.

Someone asked what a leader was. He got this answer.
A leader is someone who has followers. Some men have to get behind people and drive them. The leader sets a course and people follow him.

A steward not only represents people—he gets results through people.

Write *above* Steward:

A steward gets results
through people

Let's look at what you do as a steward.

We will let this circle represent the stewards job.

Draw circle under Steward:

A steward gets results
through people

Steward

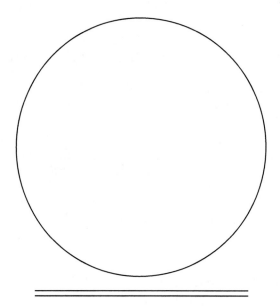

2. Let's look at the things
for which your union
holds you responsible.

* ★ Of course, our union
* ★ holds us responsible for
* ★ handling complaints and
* ★ grievances.

Write complaints
and grievances in
one segment.

---

* ★ Besides complaints and
* ★ grievances, for what
* ★ else does your union
* ★ hold you responsible?

As members suggest
kinds of union responsibilities, write the name
and outline the segment.
Write down whatever is
mentioned, but try to
include those on the
chart at right.

A steward gets results
through people

Steward

Any of the following suggestions may be offered:

    morale   working schedules
    public relations   union welfare

Leave top section of the circle unlabeled.

---

* ★ We will let this section represent all other responsibilities
* ★ of the steward.

★ 3. We won't try to define the whole job of the steward —
★ instead let's see if there is anything in common about
★ these responsibilities.

Whose grievance is the steward handling?

Do not spend too much time getting the answer, which is "People." Give it yourself if someone does not give this answer.

Put small circles in the "Complaints and Grievances" segment.

These represent people.

Who are these members?

When someone says "People," put in other circles in segment marked "Membership."

Continue until there are small circles in every segment, including the blank one.
You can say:

Who has to be instructed?

Use "who" questions.

A steward gets results through people

Steward

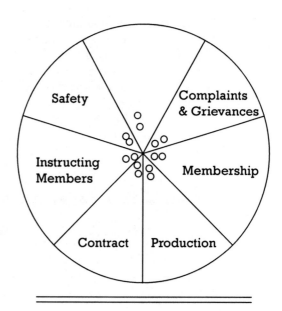

Is there any part of the steward's job which does not involve people?

No.

> Place circles in
> blank segment.

When we look at any
part of the steward's
job, we find people
in the situation.

> Enclose small circles
> in a hub.

> Erase most of the small
> circles and write
> PEOPLE inside the hub.

The steward gets results
through people.

> Point to heading.

A steward gets results
through people

Steward

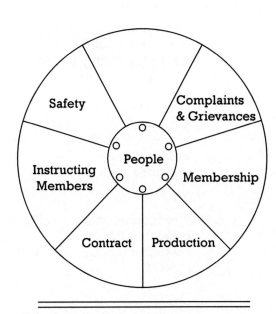

★ In order to meet these
★ responsibilities there
★ must be some
★ relationship between
★ the steward and
★ his people.

★ Let's have this line
★ represent that rela-
★ tionship.

Draw double-headed
arrow and label it
Job Relations.

Job Relations are the
everyday relations
between you and the
people you represent.

The kind of relations
you have affects the
kind of results you get.

Relations with some
are good, with others
are poor, but there
are always
relationships.

Poor relationships cause
poor results; good
relationships cause good
results.

Illustrate by use of chart.

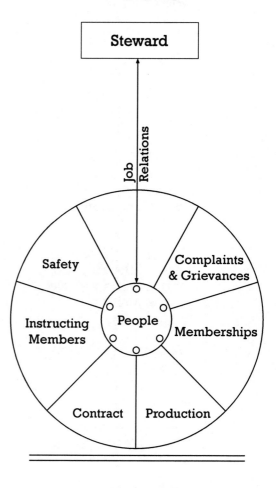

A steward gets results
through people

45 min
to here When a steward wants to meet any of these responsibilities effectively, he must have good relations with his people.

PRESENT FOUNDATIONS FOR GOOD RELATIONS

Experience shows that successful stewards use definite foundations for good relations. They find that these foundations keep the job relations line strong.

| Write on top center of board the heading: |

Foundations for Good Relations

★ 1. There are sane things that you and I as stewards can do,
★ day in and day out, about keeping the job relations line
★ in good condition.

★ For instance, we can let each member know his rights
★ and responsibilities.

| Write under heading: |

Let each member know his rights and responsibilities

Suppose a member is passed over while new men get the breaks—all because he doesn't know what the union can do for him?

Do you think that's good union job relations if a member doesn't even know what rights he has?

We know it isn't.

Don't you want to know your rights? What the union is doing for you? How your grievance is progressing?

Should a member also know his responsibilities—what the union expects of him?

I wonder if these people [point to board] would like to know their rights and responsibilities. Wouldn't that strengthen that job relations line?

★ 2. Another foundation for good job relations is
★ "Give credit when due."

| Write on board: |

Give credit when due

If you have a member who has been assigned to some committee work that doesn't particularly benefit him, and he sticks to the job and carries it through, how would it be to give him some credit.

Maybe there is someone who's never done anything outstanding, but who's always paid his dues on time and never caused any trouble. Could you give him some credit?

11

Do you think it is good job relations to give credit when due? Is that the kind of treatment you like?

I wonder if these people [point to board] wouldn't like it. Would it help the job relations line if we did give people credit when due?

★ 3. Another foundation for good relations is "Tell people in
★ advance about changes that will affect them."

| Write on board: | **Tell people in advance about changes that will affect them** |

Suppose someone tells you at quitting time that there is to be a committee meeting immediately.

Are you going to like it?

Are you going to think about your car pool?

You at least want a chance to have your say.

Would it be a good idea to tell people in advance about changes that affect them?

Do you think that would help the job relations line?

I wonder if these people [point to board] wouldn't like to know in advance about changes that affect them.

★ 4. Another foundation for good relations is "Make best use
★ of each member's ability."

| Write on board: | **Make best use of each member's ability** |

Have you ever known a member who went sour because he felt there was union work he could do if anyone asked him?

Have you ever looked around to see whether you were using the abilities the members have? Do you know what their abilities are? Make sure you don't play favorites.

I wonder if we always make best use of the ability of these people [point to board].

These foundations are important to everyone. Using them will smooth job relations and assist us as stewards to meet our responsibilities [point to board].

12

The board will look like this:

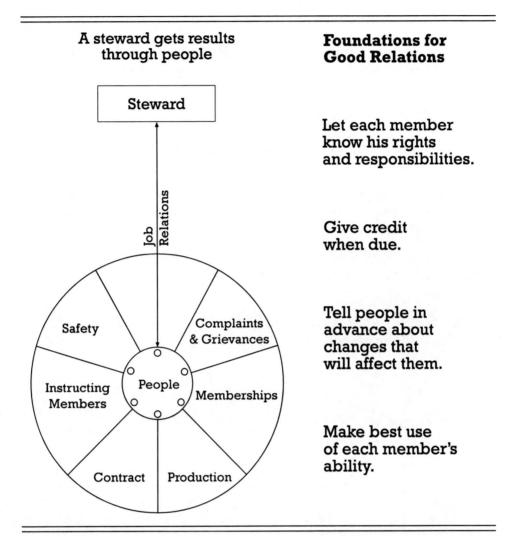

A steward gets results through people

Steward

Job Relations

Safety

Complaints & Grievances

Instructing Members

People

Memberships

Contract

Production

Foundations for Good Relations

Let each member know his rights and responsibilities.

Give credit when due.

Tell people in advance about changes that will affect them.

Make best use of each member's ability.

DEVELOP THE "INDIVIDUAL" CHART

★ Does this mean that all these people are alike? The
★ answer is no. People are different and must be
★ treated as individuals.

> Write on top right
> third of board:

**People must be treated
as individuals**

All right, no two of us are alike.

Let's pull out one of these persons and see why he is different.

> Draw a dotted line extending from one of the small circles to
> another big circle. Label it AN INDIVIDUAL. Do not erase the
> foundations.

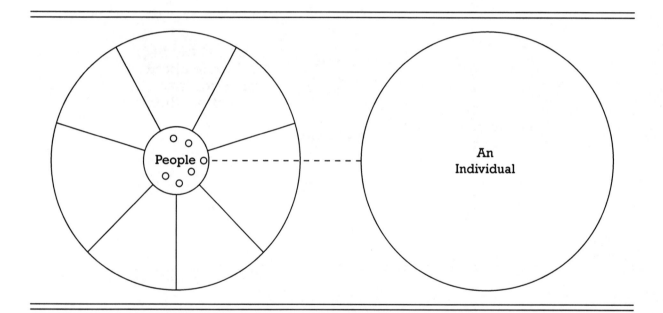

We'll let this circle represent any one of these people.

★ So let's take a look at this union member and what affects
★ him as an individual. We know that his job is a big factor.

Write "His Job" on left
one-third segment
of circle.

Now what else? What other things
affect him as an individual? What
makes one toolmaker different from
another toolmaker?

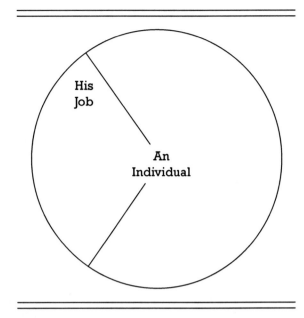

Write in interests as
members suggest.
Be sure to include
Family, Background,
and Health.

Give examples for
each, such as:

Family —
Does it make a
difference if he's
happily married?

Background —
Is there a difference
between the person
who was raised on a
farm and one who
lived in a city?

Health —
Suppose he's going
to have an operation?

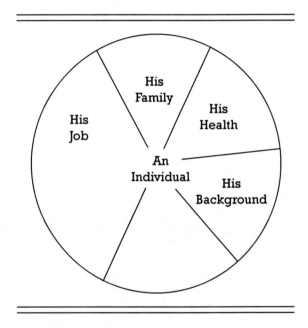

You may also get Recreation, Wages, Love Affairs, Education.

Write down not more than two or three of these.

Leave one segment for other factors.

There are, of course, many additional things which affect the individual on the job.

Leave one section unlabeled.

We will let this segment represent Other Factors.

The completed chart work will look like this:

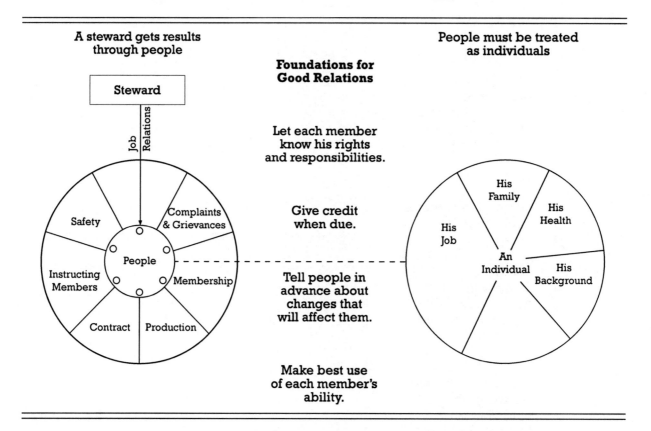

Foundations for Good Relations

A steward gets results through people

People must be treated as individuals

Steward

Job Relations

Safety — Complaints & Grievances

People

Instructing Members — Membership

Contract — Production

Let each member know his rights and responsibilities.

Give credit when due.

Tell people in advance about changes that will affect them.

Make best use of each member's ability.

An Individual — His Family, His Health, His Job, His Background

All of these really affect the individual who belongs to your union.

He doesn't leave part of himself at home when he comes to work or to a union meeting.

The things noted in the circle make individuals different.

You need to know this person as a separate individual because he is different and that affects him on the job.

Summarize the chart.

- A steward gets results through people.

- By using the foundations we can improve our relations with people.

- A steward must treat his people as individuals.

1 hr
5 min
to here

These are the basis for good job relations.

But their use will not prevent all problems.

Allow
5 min

DEFINE A "PROBLEM"

What do we mean by a problem?

★ A problem is ANYTHING THE STEWARD
★ *HAS TO TAKE ACTION ON.*

This may include handling a complaint, or any small incident you have to do something about.

Changes, interruptions, and failures <u>do</u> occur; and situations do arise. These cause problems.

Each steward needs <u>skill</u> in understanding individuals, sizing up situations, and working with people.

We are going to get experience in using a <u>method</u> for meeting problems.

What we are going to be working on is the relation between you and the people you represent.

This relationship is the same whether you are working on a complaint, a grievance, getting dues paid, or any of your other responsibilities.

These relations are important.

They affect the job.

Good relations give you good results.

1 hr
10 min
to here

Poor relations give you poor results.

Conditions change all the time—so do relations.

17

INTRODUCE T.W.I. METHOD

> Tell the problem about Mike.
> Do not read. The trainer must be able to *tell this well*, changing
> no ideas, but using words natural to him.

1. Let us take a look at the action of one steward—something that happened in a war production plant.

One day the steward walked into the pay office and saw Mike sitting there. He asked Mike what he was doing and Mike said he was waiting for his pay-off as he had been fired.

It seemed a plant protection man had reported him for being asleep in the warehouse. The steward asked him if he had been asleep, and Mike said he had—for three hours. Mike said he needed his job. Now the steward knew that Mike had a bad record and that held been warned by the supervisor.

Only two months ago the union had told him they were fed up and couldn't keep on interceding for him forever. Other people had complained about his loafing. He had been found sleeping before by the plant protection department.

The steward decided that he couldn't do anything more for him and said "So long, Mike—better luck next place."

> Erase charts from board.

2. | Discuss. |

This steward had a problem, didn't he?

How do you think he handled it?

★ Just what was this steward trying to accomplish?

> Get the group to say:

He wanted to get Mike a square deal.

> If necessary, ask:

What is this steward's responsibility to Mike?

> If the group tends to agree with the steward, remind them that what he wanted was a square deal.

18

But he made no attempt to do anything about it.

Would you have taken this action?

> Do not let this go into extensive discussion.

> If these points do not come out in the discussion, make them
> yourself:

He made no attempt to find out why Mike was asleep.

The steward jumped to the conclusion that Mike was, after all,
just an irresponsible person.

Mike had been around long enough to know better.

3. Tell what happened next.

The next day people in the department came up and told the steward that Mike was sick the day before. He decided to rest a bit and went to sleep. He'd been very steady and reliable since his soldier son-in-law was killed two months ago. He needed all he could make because he had his daughter's children to support. Mike was sick yesterday and he was still sick that day.

4. Discuss.

Do these additional facts throw more light?

Mike had had a good record for a while, but the steward didn't
think of that.

The steward couldn't think of anything good about Mike.

Mike had gone to sleep because he was sick.

Let's look at what the steward did from three angles:

How would Mike feel toward the steward?

How did the other people in the department feel about
the way he treated Mike?

What did it do to Union Relations?

It was the wrong thing to do on all three counts.

5. Is there a way to avoid mistakes like this?

What could Mike's steward have done first?

> If someone suggests "Talk with Mike" or "Give him a chance to explain" ask, "Do you mean, 'Get the facts'?"

Write on board:

Get the Facts

It certainly is important to "*Be sure you have the whole story.*"

Then what would he do with these facts?

Get group to say and write on board:

Weigh and Decide

Aren't we all tempted to jump to conclusions?

After deciding, what would he do next?

Get group to say and write on board:

Take Action

It's easy to pass the buck, isn't it?

After you take action, is it a good idea to see how it came out?

Write on board:

Check Results

Did Joe's supervisor's action help production?

Leave steps on board.

HAND OUT CARDS, SUMMARIZE 4-STEP METHOD

Distribute cards individually—STRESS THEIR IMPORTANCE.

> Read the "How to Handle a Problem" side of the card and comment as follows:

★ <u>Determine Objective.</u>

   We agreed that the steward wanted to get a square deal for Mike.

   An objective is something to shoot for. It's what you want to accomplish.

★ <u>1. Get the Facts.</u>

   We said that Mike's steward did not get the facts.

   ★ <u>Review the record</u> (source of facts).

      The steward recalled Mike's previous bad record but evidently overlooked his recent good record.

      All records are not paper records. You include what you know about someone.

   ★ <u>Find out what union and plant rules and customs apply</u> (source of facts).

      There were rules in both the plant and the union.

      There are some things that are accepted as what you do in the union and plant. Some are written and they're rules. But the unwritten customs are just as strong. You also have to consider any precedents which have been established.

   ★ <u>Talk with individuals concerned</u> (source of facts).

      Mike's steward did not take the time to talk with Mike or anyone else in the department.

   ★ <u>Get opinions and feelings</u> (source of facts).

      This steward just didn't get the opinions of any of these people and he didn't think how they might feel. Remember that what a person feels or thinks, right or wrong, is a fact to him and must be considered as such.

   ★ <u>Be sure you have the whole story</u> (a caution).

      You pointed out that the steward didn't have the whole story—he did not know what had happened in Mike's family or that the man was ill.

21

★ 2. <u>Weigh and Decide</u>.

Did the steward do a good job on this step?

★ <u>Fit the facts together.</u>

Look for gaps and contradictions. In this one there were gaps, but the steward didn't try to fill them in. Why Mike was asleep is the big gap in the facts.

★ <u>Consider their bearing on each other.</u>

This steward only looked at the bearing of some facts on each other. He overlooked Mike's current good record and decided that he was back in the old rut.

★ <u>What possible actions are there?</u>

This steward thought there was only one thing to do—turn Mike down. There is usually more than one possible action if we stop to weigh the facts.

★ <u>Check union and management practices and policies.</u>

The steward has to know the ground rules. He has to know whether his action is within company policies and practices and within union practices and policies.

★ <u>Consider objective and effect on individual, group, union, and production.</u>

Mike's steward did not consider the effect of his action on his objective, on Mike, on the other people, on the union, or on production.

★ <u>Don't jump to conclusions</u> (a caution).

Do you think that Mike's steward jumped to a conclusion?

★ 3. <u>Take Action.</u>

★ <u>Are you going to handle this yourself?</u>

It was up to Mike's steward to handle this problem.

★ <u>Do you need help in handling?</u>

Sometimes we can get help from another department—from an officer or from the district office.

★ <u>Should you refer this?</u>

You have to decide whether a problem is beyond

22

your own authority for action.

★ Watch the timing of your action.

The timing does influence the effectiveness of what you do. Think of the effectiveness, not just your convenience.

★ Don't pass the buck (a caution).

I guess we all know what this means—and we can say for Mike's steward that he didn't pass the buck. He thought he knew enough about this to turn Mike down.

★ 4. Check Results.

It is always important to consider how you are going to follow up. This steward didn't have to check results— they came right to him.

★ How soon will you follow up?

You make your first check as soon as you can reasonably expect results.

★ How often will you need to check?

Sometimes you keep an eye on something for quite a while just to make sure that your action hasn't caused another problem. The way the steward treated Mike caused plenty of other problems.

★ Watch for changes in attitudes and relationships within the union and toward management.

You have to look at what your action did to the group as well as to the individual person concerned.

★ Did your action strengthen Union Job Relations?

We've seen that this steward fell down straight through because he failed to get the facts—he didn't even consider all the facts he had, so his action was wrong, and he got poor results.

Ask stewards to turn the cards over. Read the "Foundations for Good Relations," commenting as follows:

★ Let each member know his rights and responsibilities.

Wouldn't it prevent a lot of problems if every member understood?

★ <u>Tell him what the union can do for him</u> (action point).

This is a never-ending job.

★ <u>Tell him what the union expects from him</u> (action point).

This is important for every steward to remember.

★ <u>Give credit when due.</u>

Don't we all respond to recognition?

★ <u>Look for extra or unusual performance</u> (action point).

Sometimes it's the man who's unusually reliable who deserves some form of credit.

★ <u>Tell him while "it's hot"</u> (action point).

Don't get so busy that you overlook some simple thanks right when they are due.

★ <u>Tell people in advance about changes that will affect them.</u>

All of us have to get used to changes.

★ <u>Tell them why if possible</u> (action point).

Give reasons, not arbitrary decisions.

★ <u>Get them to accept the change</u> (action point).

Help people to understand.

★ <u>Make best use of each member's ability.</u>

Won't this help you do a better job?

★ <u>Look for ability not now being used</u> (action point).

Are you sure you know just what abilities there are in your group?

★ <u>Never stand in a man's way</u> (action point).

Has this ever caused trouble for you?

★ These are the basic rules for good relations. They will
★ do a job for you if you use them. If they are used they
★ will keep many problems from coming up.

Remember that you need to treat all people as individuals.

These foundations will smooth union job relations but they will not insure you against problems.

We have stewards because there are problems to handle.

We are stewards because the union has designated us to handle these problems.

SUMMARIZE

1. Good stewardship includes two points:

Working with the individuals you represent in a way which makes everyday relationships smooth and prevents many problems. This is covered by the Foundations.

Handling problems that do arise is covered by the 4-step method.

2. The steward's job can't be run from a set of rules any more than you can learn to play baseball from a book. You can read about pitching a curve but you can't get the ball to curve until you have practiced.

3. Conditions do change; interruptions do occur; problems do come up. The Foundations and this 4-step method will help you to handle these problems. This is a pattern to follow.

This method applies whether there is a Wagner Act or not, whether you are dealing with a man or a woman, negro or white, Republican or Democrat.

Why is this so? Because people are people once you get under their skins, regardless of race or color.

DISCUSS HOW PROBLEMS COME UP

★ Let's look at the way PROBLEMS come up.

★ 1. If you're on the watch in your department you'll be
★ tipped off when you notice changes in people's work or
★ attitudes. Suppose a man suddenly gets quarrelsome with
★ everyone around him. That's a problem, isn't it?
★ Effective stewards get in on these early.

★ 2. Or, you may even have a situation to size up before it
★ happens. The union may change a policy, or suppose
★ management is going to bring a group of women into a
★ department where there have been only men. You may
★ want to do some preventive work and size up that situation
★ in advance so that you won't have a problem to handle
★ later.

★ 3. Sometimes they "come to you." A member may ask for a
★ rate increase or a transfer, or he may have a problem or
★ question.

25

★ 4. Others, you "run into." Suppose you tell a member to
★ abide by union policy, and he won't do it. Or perhaps it's a
★ member who refuses to pay dues.

CONSIDER STEWARD'S PROBLEMS ON THE JOB

1. | Distribute problem sheets. |

Some of the same problems come to all stewards.

Maybe you have all of these—or none.

| Ask group to check problem sheets. |

| Read five or six out loud—discuss, not at length. |

| Let the group read, all the way through. |

In this group we are going to be working on your own problems—the things you have to do something about.

| Comment on number of problems group has. |

2. | Practice in following sessions.
See Tips for Trainers. |

Each of you will have a chance to bring in a problem during these sessions.

We will work on these problems to develop our skill in the use of the 4-step method.

UNION JOB RELATIONS SITUATIONS AND PROBLEMS

Someone kicks about working conditions.
Complaints about slow handling of grievances.
Member wants to change jobs often.
Lack of interest in union activities.
Worker violates union contract.

Member feels he is being pushed.
Member unreasonable in demands.
Man goes over your head to complain.
Member takes chances at work.
Worker fails to come to work every day.

Member resents changes.
Worker dissatisfied with union agreement.
Worker irritable and touchy.
Operator refuses to do certain work.
Careless with materials and equipment.

Member gets discouraged learning job.
Former steward causing trouble.
Member wants more money.
Employee kicks when not promoted.
Pay differential causes trouble.

Plant is going to start hiring women, or negroes.
Drop in overall production.
Friction between shifts.
Members fail to attend meetings.
Defeated candidate not cooperating.

We *are not* going to criticize the steward or pass judgment on his action.

When you bring in your problem,

REMEMBER:

★ Our definition of a problem is something the steward has to
★ take action on. This includes recommending action or
★ sending a complaint or grievance on to a further step, or
★ telling someone he has no basis for his complaint and that
★ no action can be taken.

★ It must involve you and the people you represent—other-
★ wise we may not have all the facts or know the individuals
★ concerned.

★ You may bring in a problem that you have handled recent-
★ ly. These problems are good because the facts are easily
★ recalled.

★ You may bring in a problem on which you have not as yet
★ taken action. Pending problem are always good.

★ You will help all of us if you will bring some problems that
★ didn't turn out quite right, so we can take a look at why
★ they turned out the way they did.

★ It will also be helpful if you bring in some problems of rel-
★ ationships entirely within the union, which do not involve
★ management or the plant. But remember, it still must be
★ something you can do something about.

Please do not bring in the most involved problem that you have run into in all of your years of union experience. When problems are pretty big, or involved, most of us usually say—"This is a pretty tough one. I'd better get the facts and weigh them carefully."

Stewards tell us that they usually go a bit sour with the smaller problems as they appear to be so insignificant that they are prone not to get the facts, jump to conclusions, etc.

We want to get experience and practice them so that we will instinctively think through small problems, so that these small problems will be handled satisfactorily and forgotten.

Some stewards say that most all of their large problems result from small problems which were poorly handled. If there is a little blaze, we usually can put it out with a cup of water, but if it develops into a big blaze, then we have to call out the fire departments from neighboring towns.

Sometimes we overlook the little things. You give someone union work to do and he just doesn't do it.

You have a member who doesn't get to work on time.

These small incidents are problems.

Because of our time limit we have to have short and relatively simple problems. This is necessary because we are going to apply the entire method, not just the beginning of it. We can learn the method just as well on short problems as on long ones. If we get practice and form a habit, it will be easier to use the method on more involved problems, and it will make the handling of those problems shorter.

Remember that the steward does much preventive work by handling his problems while they are new and small rather than waiting until they are older and more complicated.

3. Do any of you have any problems, like these on the problem sheet perhaps, facing you? I mean some you have to handle yourself? Well, will you ....and ....tell us about one at the next meeting, just as I told you about Mike, so we all can take a look at them together?

Explain procedure for handling stewards' problems.

4. I'm going to bring in a problem too.

Our purpose in all these problems is to *get practice* in the use of the *4-step method*. We only acquire skill through practice.

5. You can begin to use these foundations and the four steps right away—on the job.

That's where this plan pays dividends.

Thank group for interest and participation.

Clear the board.

IMPORTANCE OF GETTING THE FACTS

REVIEW 4-STEP METHOD

1. Briefly make appropriate opening comments.

Let's take a look at our 4-step method of handling problems.

2. What are the four steps a good steward follows when he takes action on a problem?

Draw from group and place in upper right hand corner of board:

1. **Get the Facts**
2. **Weigh and Decide**
3. **Take Action**
4. **Check Results**

3. We are setting up a pattern here. We handle these situations in slow motion, in order to get a closer look at them. Even though this method happens more quickly on the job, you still go through the same steps.

5 min
to here

4. This may seem to take time—but if it saves time in the long run, isn't it surely worth it?

Allow
35 min

DEVELOP ABILITY IN USING THE METHOD by presenting and discussing the Tom problem

1. Focus attention on importance of Step 1—Get the Facts.

In the use of this method, Step 1 is basic, because the success of Steps 2, 3, and 4, depends on getting all the facts.

Underline Step 1

1. Get the Facts

In some problems ALL THE FACTS are not obtained until personal opinions and feelings are considered. These personal opinions and feelings must be considered as facts. What a worker thinks—right or wrong—is a fact to him and must be considered as such.

I am now going to tell you about a problem in which a steward talked with a man and, by getting his opinions and feelings, obtained important facts.

The purpose in relating this particular problem is to stress not only the importance of getting the facts, but also to give us an opportunity to see exactly how this steward talked with this member in order to get personal opinions and feelings.

This problem is one where what is said—and how it is said—is very important. I'm going to read this to you so we'll get just what was said by both of them.

2. Read the problem. MAKE IT LIVE. DO NOT READ IN A MONOTONE.

A steward is out in the shop and notices a workman is reaching into a machine. In this particular plant the bargaining agreement between the union and management had created a safety committee which made the steward jointly responsible with the departmental foreman for the prevention of accidents within their departments.

Steward calls out: Tom, I've told you to shut off that machine when you take off the guard.

Trainer Comment: The steward is mad. He's apparently warned Tom before.

Tom yells back: If you want to report me, why don't you do it instead of nagging at me all the time.

Trainer Comment: Tom is mad too.

Steward: Keep your shirt on! I don't want to get you in trouble. I just don't want you to get your hand mashed. The number of times that machine has to be adjusted makes me think there must be something wrong with it.

Tom: Well, I'm not going to take any more panning.

Trainer Comment: The steward is certainly facing a problem and here is what went through his mind very quickly before he took any action.

Steward: Now, let's see. I've know Tom a long time. He's been one of the best men in the department and a good union member. But lately he's always in trouble, and the superintendent is riding the union about accidents. Tom is as reckless as the devil about his machine, but that isn't all. Yesterday I had to get after him about his dues and he hasn't been to a union meeting in months. What's happened to Tom? I guess I have been on his neck a lot, but it was always something that had to be done. And we can't have him taking chances the way he does.

> Trainer Comment: Do you notice how this problem came up? There had been a change in Tom, but the steward didn't get into the problem then. He waited until it burst in his face.

Steward: Suppose we get together later and talk this over. If there is something wrong with that machine we'll report it.

> Trainer Comment: Why do you think the steward didn't talk to him then? Do you think it would have done any good to stay there right then and argue with him? He isn't going to talk in the department or while Tom is mad.

That noon the steward watched for Tom and took his lunch over and sat down beside him.

Steward: Hello, Tom. Now, Tom, I guess you think I've been riding you. I don't want to do anything like that. I felt I had to yell at you today because you were doing something dangerous. And there've been a couple of other things lately that the union just can't put up with. Every time I see you taking a chance that might cause trouble, I've got to stop you. When you don't pay your dues, why then I've got to say something about that too.

Now is there something the matter with the machine? I know you're always raising the guard and reaching into it. If there is something wrong with that machine, I want to get it reported.

> Trainer Comment: What is the steward doing here? The steward is trying the obvious thing first—to see if the trouble is connected with the machine.

Tom: Well, if you think I'm going to run over to that switch and pull it, and hang the "don't touch" sign on it—you're just crazy. You're yelling now about how little I get done. If I had to spend half of my time turning that switch off and on, I wouldn't get anything done. And the other day you said there'd been a report that I was letting parts that were below standard go through. Well, if I didn't fix that machine they'd all be below standard.

> Trainer Comment: Tom isn't going to make it easy, is he? The steward could have cut in there and told him it wouldn't take half the time to turn off the switch. Here again he could have <u>argued</u>, but he had gotten Tom off to the side because he wanted to talk with him, so he wasn't going to <u>interrupt</u> him.

Steward: Now, Tom, there's more to it than breaking a safety rule. There's a reason behind that rule. You're apt to get your hand mashed.

Tom: And that'd cost the company money, wouldn't it? And then they'd razz the union.

31

> Trainer Comment: The steward might think that Tom was sore at the company about money—or would that be jumping to a conclusion?

Steward: Oh, sure it would cost the company money and they ride us plenty about accidents. But have we made you think that's all we're interested in?

Tom: Well, that's all that counts with some people.

> Trainer Comment: He's bitter about something.

Steward: It'd cost us a good man, and that's a hard thing to replace.

Tom: Well, not everybody feels that way.

> Trainer Comment: He seems to be thinking about the importance of money to some people. The steward has a cue here—will he follow it up? Tom has been pretty hard to talk to. What does the steward have to follow up from here?
>
> Do not allow extended discussion. If the group does not make the point, say that Tom seems to be thinking about the importance of money to somebody.

Steward: Why are you so strong on the money angle? You're doing all right that way, aren't you? Seems to me you told me last spring you were going to build on that land of yours out on the pike. When are you getting married? When you have a wife she won't want you to take chances.

Tom: Oh—nobody cares if I do get a hand cut off.

Steward: Your girl would care.

Tom: I don't have a girl any more.

Steward: I'm sorry, Tom. I just wanted to get you thinking of what an injury to you might mean to somebody else.

Tom: Well, it doesn't mean anything to anyone now. Nothing about me would hurt her. Why, she knew I was going to start to build, but she married someone else. So, all I have is a half-finished house. And that's all I've got to show for it. Nobody cares what happens to me any more. And I don't need to try to make any more money, or save it either. It changes a lot of things.

> Trainer Comment: This takes careful handling. The steward wants to get Tom back to normal production; he wants to stay on good terms with Tom. Now the steward has a chance to make a speech—he could tell Tom he was lucky to get rid of her, but he's going to listen to Tom, and not do all the talking himself.

32

Steward: A blow like that's bad, and it's no use saying it isn't. But some times you just have to take it on the chin. Some things can be fixed up, though. And I wish you'd see your way clear to helping me figure out what is wrong with the way that line is running. It's getting you in trouble, and that gets me in on it too.

I can see why you have gotten a bit careless about taking chances. But I know you wouldn't have had to take those chances unless something else had been wrong. Now, is the machine worn? Does it need overhauling? How are the tools?

> Trainer Comment: There seems to be two thing to look at: (1) the man and (2) the machine.

Tom: No, it isn't the machine. The parts aren't coming through the same as they used to. There's a burr left on them; and after so many have gone through, well, I just have to clean the machine out.

> Handle this problem according to standard procedure.

3. Just what is the steward trying to accomplish?

> Get from group and place on board:

**Just what is this steward trying to accomplish?
To make Tom a safe worker.**

4. What are the facts?

> Get facts from group and put on board briefly. See that these are included, but not necessarily in this order.

Facts

**Was a good worker
Quality and quantity down
Broke safety rule
Careless
Warned before
Talked back
Stopped attending
    union meetings
Back on dues
Lost his girl
Felt nobody cared
Burr on parts**

> Check subheads of Step 1. USE CARD.

> Be sure that you leave group with the realization that the steward got three very important facts because he talked with the individual to get their opinions and feelings.

5. ⌐ Consider Step 2, according to standard procedure. ⌐

⌐ Get possible actions
from group.

Some may be —
Warn about safety rules.
Recommend
 penalty layoff.
Report bad parts.
Tell him losing girl isn't
your fault. ⌐

Weigh and decide

Possible Actions

—————————

—————————

—————————

⌐ Test possible actions against objective and probable
effect on the individual—group—union—production. ⌐

6. Now let us see what happened in this particular problem.

⌐ Continue to read the problem. ⌐

Steward: I can see why that would cause you trouble. Now, I'm sorry about
your tough luck, but I do thank you for helping me. I'm going to report the
bad parts to the supervisor.

⌐ Trainer Comment: Throughout, the steward had listened sym-
pathetically to Tom; he had encouraged and helped him to talk
about the things that were important to him. Now that he had
reached something specific (bad parts) he is going to talk to
management about it.

Later the steward goes into the supervisor's office. ⌐

Steward: I want to talk to you about the parts the department is getting from
the punch press. They're not coming through clean. There's a good operator
on the line and it's making it pretty dangerous for him if he tries to keep up
production.

7. What were the additional facts that the steward got by talking with Tom and getting his opinions and feelings?

⌐ Point out on board THE
ADDITIONAL FACTS: ⌐

**Lost his girl
Felt nobody cared
Burrs on parts**

34

8. The steward looked at all the facts and he felt he had a complete story.

He found out why Tom was off the beam.

Doesn't this indicate that sometimes an addition of one more fact will preclude or suggest a possible action? Do you think we would have had the same possible actions if these facts had been missing?

9. What action did he take?

Help group give
supervisor's action.
Write this action on
the board:

ACTION

Told Tom he was sorry
Asked Tom's help
Reported faulty parts

What facts did this steward use in arriving at this decision?

Handle Step 3 as in the standard procedure.

Let's look at Step 3.

Are you going to handle this yourself?

It was this steward's problem.

He had the responsibility to take some action.

Need help?

Yes, he got Tom's help—no outside help was necessary.

Refer to someone else?

To get good parts—but didn't tell Tom's trouble.

Timing?

Tom's steward didn't lose any time in acting.

Stress importance of good timing.

10. Handle Step 4 as in the standard procedure.

How soon do you think he'll follow up? More than once?

What will he look for?

Do you think Tom's steward will accomplish his objective?

Did this steward use the 4-step method up to now?

11. ⎡ Conclusion to the Tom problem. ⎤

You remember the purpose of this problem was to stress not only the importance of getting the facts, but also to see how this steward got personal opinions and feelings. You can see what might have happened if this steward had not decided to get more facts before he took his action.

Do you think Tom's steward was justified in getting him to talk about his personal affairs? This depends on the individual and the problem. This steward knew this individual well enough to talk personally with him.

Did you ever have a man go sour when something happened in his family? He brought what happened outside of work into the plant with him—just as Tom did. That's why the steward has to concern himself with personal feelings.

Did you notice that when Tom's steward talked to the supervisor he didn't reveal the personal information he had about Tom? He could have said, "I have a jilted guy down here," but he said, "I have a good worker down here."

⎡ Clear board, except question and steps. ⎤

REMEMBER WE SAID THAT OPINIONS AND FEELINGS

are hard to get

We all can learn and develop this skill. Once this skill is acquired it becomes a useful tool for a steward.

⎡ Write on board: ⎤

How to get opinions and feelings

1. Just how did Tom's steward find out about Tom's opinions and feelings?

His steward could have argued with Tom about its taking him half his time to turn off the switch. Is anything ever satisfactorily settled by an argument? Our first tip, then, is "Don't argue."

⎡ Write on board: ⎤

Don't argue

36

2. It took some encouragement to get Tom to talk about what seemed important to him, didn't it? The steward had to help him say what was wrong. The tip then is to, "Encourage him to talk about what is important to him."

Write on board:	Encourage him to talk about what is important to him

3. If you are telling a story and someone interrupts you, do you feel like continuing it? After Tom started talking did the steward interrupt him? Our tip is "Don't interrupt."

Write on board:	Don't interrupt

4. Could the steward have spoiled everything by jumping to the conclusion that Tom was sore about money? The tip is, "Don't jump to conclusions."

Write on board:	Don't jump to conclusions

5. The steward had a chance to make a couple of speeches, didn't he—on safety—on how lucky he was to get rid of the girl? You will notice he didn't do all the talking himself. The tip is "Don't do all the talking yourself."

Write on board:	Don't do all the talking yourself

6. Was Tom's steward a good listener? If you want to get opinions and feelings you have to listen, don't you? Our tip is, "Listen."

Write on board:	Listen

Bring out to the group the importance of using these tips.

Clear the board—except question and steps.

STEWARDS' PROBLEMS

Handle 2 problems.
35 minutes each.
Standard Procedure.

MAKE SURE 3 PROBLEMS WILL BE PRESENTED AT NEXT SESSION

1. I'll bring in another problem at the next session.

2. Will all of you have one ready?

You can bring in a problem you want to size up to try to take some preventive action.

Or you can bring one that's on your hands right now.

Or perhaps you have just finished a problem we can consider.

But we do set up these requirements:

★ It must be something between you and the people you
★ represent.

★ It must be a problem which you have to handle, not
★ someone else's job.

★ You must have the necessary information about the
★ employee or employees involved—age, length of service,
★ experience, etc.

.... and .... brought in the kind of problems we have to live with. That's the kind we want.

3. Do all of you have a problem that you can tell us about to practice our 4-step method?

If any member of group says he does not have a problem, use the problem sheet again.

Remind the group that, to receive a certificate, each member must bring in a problem, participate satisfactorily, and attend all sessions.

Clear the board.

Just what is this

steward trying

to accomplish?

To make Tom a
safe worker.

Facts

Was a good worker
Quality and quantity down
Broke safety rule
Careless
Warned before
Talked back
Stopped attending
    union meetings
Back on dues
Lost his girl
Felt nobody cared
Burr on parts

1. Get the Facts
2. Weigh and Decide
3. Take Action
4. Check Results

Weigh and Decide

Possible Actions

    Warn about safety rules
    Recommend
        penalty layoff
    Report bad parts
    Tell him losing girl isn't
        your fault

ACTION

Told Tom he was sorry
Asked Tom's help
Reported faulty parts

STANDARD PROCEDURE

1. Ask steward to tell problem.

Head of table. Does this involve you and somebody whom you represent? Have you taken action? Tell up to final action.

2. How problems come up.

Where appropriate, stress; you sensed, or anticipated a change.

3. Get objective.

Get from steward:
Something to shoot at. May be changed.
What do you want to have happen here?
Does this problem affect the group?
What net result do you want after you have taken action?

Get group agreement.

4. Get Facts.

Steward first, as he recalls them offhand.
Review subheads with steward—USE CARDS.
Get additional facts from group—USE CARDS.

5. Weigh and Decide.

Fit facts—Look for gaps and contradictions with group.
Possible Action:
What facts used?—From steward.
Check practices and policies with steward.
Check objective first with group, then last with steward.
Check probable effect on individual, group, union, and production, with steward.

6. Balance of Case.

Facts used (from steward).

7. Check Step 3.

Subheads—with steward.
Why?—How?—Timing?

8. Check Step 4.

Subheads—with steward.
When?—How often?—What?

9. Check Objective.

Steward.

10. Foundations (if applicable)

Steward.

(Thank steward and clear board except questions and steps.)

WEIGHING AND DECIDING

Before session starts, place on board:	Just what is this steward trying to accomplish?	1. Get the Facts 2. Weigh and Decide 3. Take Action 4. Check Results

Time
Table
Allow
5 min

REVIEW 4-STEP METHOD

1. Now do we all have our cards? Suppose we take a look at the 4-step method. In our last session the problem I presented about Tom, who lost his girl, stressed the importance of getting the facts, with particular reference to personal opinions and feelings.

We looked at the way a steward got the facts in order to make a good decision. It takes time to do this, but in the long run it does save time, doesn't it?

2. It is interesting to notice that a similar method is used by professional people. For instance, let us see how a doctor handles his problem.

Step 1—Does the doctor get the facts?

Record—personal history—blood pressure—temperature.

Rules and customs—medical knowledge—practice—ethics.

Talk—to get more facts, confidential.

Opinions and feelings—very important.

Step 2—Diagnosis.

Fit facts together—assemble facts.

Consider bearing on each other—symptoms.

Possible actions—medicine, operate.

Check practices and policies—must comply with laws.

Effect on individual—group—contagion.

Don't jump to conclusions—careful diagnosis.

Step 3—Treatment.

Take action—prescribe, operate.

Handle yourself?—his specialty.

Help in handling—nurse, technician.

Refer to supervisor—more experienced doctor, specialist.

Doctors don't lose face in doing this.

Timing—importance of timing.

Don't pass the buck.

Step 4—Check results—X-ray.

How soon—depends on case.

How often—it differs.

Watch for—changes in condition.

This method we have been talking about works in other professions, doesn't it? The doctor in an emergency of life or death still takes time for all these steps.

3. Now let's turn the spotlight on Step 2 of our method, Weigh and Decide.

Good decisions must have a good foundation. You must have the facts.

They must be weighed.

⌐ Underline Step 2. ⌐

2. Weigh and decide

PRESENT THE PROBLEM ABOUT THE OLD HAND

1. Let's take a look at something that happened in a war plant and particularly at the decision the steward made since we are today stressing Step 2.

⌐ Tell the opening of the problem. ⌐

There was an old hand who was transferred into this department because he had been injured. He was breaking a safety rule when he was hurt, but the union had taken up the problem and got the transfer to a job he could do even if he did have a bad foot. That meant, of course, that he got full pay instead of workmen's compensation.

Now the old hand never showed that he appreciated what had been done. The steward couldn't get any cooperation from him at all. The supervisor complained about him all the time, too.

Everybody could see that he was loafing on the job. His foot was healed and he kept hounding the steward about getting transferred back to his old job. The steward was fed up.

One day the old hand yelled clear across the shop at the steward. "When are you going to get me my transfer? What do you think I pay dues for? Not to keep people like you in office!"

Everyone was listening. The steward was sore. He decided it was time to do something about this problem.

2. Comment on how problem came up—ran into it, but steward had warning—the old hand had been complaining for some time.

3. Get the objective from group and put on board:

Eliminate trouble in the group

4. Continue with standard procedure to get these facts, but not necessarily in this order. Place on board.

Facts

Old hand — injured
Broke rule — hurt foot
Union assisted in transfer
    — full pay
Union action not appreciated
Uncooperative with steward
Loafed on job
Foot O.K. — wanted transfer
Steward fed up
Made a scene
Steward sore
Everyone listening

Review the card, subheads Step 1.

5. STEP 2—FOLLOW STANDARD PROCEDURE.

Get possible actions
from group.
Some may be:

Ask that man be
transferred
Ignore
Get other union
members to help
Calm down, then rem-
ind him what union
has done for him
Tell him to quit if he
doesn't like it

Weigh and decide

Possible Actions

_____

_____

_____

_____

Test possible actions against objective and probable effect on
the individual—group—union—and production.

6. Now let's finish the problem and see what actually happened.

Well, the steward let him have it. He told the old hand just exactly how lucky he
was and how much the union had already done for him and that he wasn't going to do
anything more.

But the old hand didn't let that end it. He went to his old boss and that supervisor
took it up. The old hand didn't even know that the transfer had been to get him full pay.
His old boss was glad to have him back, and fixed it up.

Then the president of the local heard about it—and he told that steward a few things.
This old hand was one of the original members of the local, and he felt the younger
members owed him quite a lot.

7. Get additional
facts from group
and list on board
under facts.

Facts

Founder of local union
Didn't know union had helped
him get full pay

8. Continue with standard procedure.

Write on the blackboard:

ACTION

Told him union had done all
it would for him

44

Have group identify the facts which the steward used when he came to the decision that he wasn't going to do anything for the old hand.

Also have group identify the facts which were not used in the final decision.

Does this make a reasonable case for the old hand?

Does this indicate to you that, if the steward had intelligently weighed all the facts which he had, he would not have refused to help him?

Stress to the group that the steward gave weight to only a very few of the facts which he had as a basis for his decision.

Other stewards, by giving more weight to the facts which he missed, might arrive at other decisions, such as those already listed on the blackboard under Possible Actions.

9. Comment on Step 3 subheads—standard procedure. Have group follow cards.

Handle yourself?—This was his problem.

Help in handling?—Didn't ask for help.

Refer?—Didn't refer.

Timing of action?—Was this the time to take action?

10. Comment on Step 4 subheads—standard Procedure. Use cards.

How soon? How often?

> This steward did not have to check up on the results of his action. They were not satisfactory to the old hand and he went over the steward's head.

Changes in attitudes and relationships?

> This steward lost standing with the individual, the group, and his union.

11. Check objective.

12. Use foundation points as in standard procedure.

Hit hard on "Make Best Use of Each Person's Ability." (prevention)

13. It is interesting to note in this problem that even though the steward did not have all the facts, nevertheless he did not do a good job of weighing the facts which he had.

Perhaps if he had given more weight to several seemingly unimportant facts, he would not have taken the action which he did.

*35 min
to here*

Clear the blackboard except question and steps.

---

*Allow
1 hr
25 min*
STEWARDS' PROBLEMS

Handle 3 problems
2 problems 30 min. each
1 problem 25 min.
Standard Procedure

MAKE SURE THREE PROBLEMS WILL BE PRESENTED AT NEXT SESSION.

*2 hrs
to here*
Re-emphasize what you mean by a problem; how they come up. Remind group that, to receive a certificate, each steward must bring in a problem, participate satisfactorily, and attend all five sessions.

Clear the board.

Just what is this

supervisor trying

to accomplish?

Eliminate trouble
in the group.

Facts

Old hand — injured
Broke rule — hurt foot
Union assisted in transfer
   — full pay
Union action not appreciated
Uncooperative with steward
Loafed on job
Foot O.K. — wanted transfer
Steward fed up
Made a scene
Steward sore
Everyone listening

1. Get the Facts
2. Weigh and Decide
3. Take Action
4. Check Results

Weigh and Decide

Possible Actions

Ask that man be
   transfered
Ignore
Get other union
   members to help
Calm down, then rem-
   ind him what union
   has done for him
Tell him to quit if he
   doesn't like it

ACTION

Told him union had done all
   it would for him

STANDARD PROCEDURE

1. Ask steward to tell problem.

   Head of table. Does this involve you and somebody whom you represent? Have you taken action? Tell up to final action.

2. How problems come up.

   Where appropriate, stress; you sensed, or anticipated a change.

3. Get objective.

   Get from steward:
   Something to shoot at. May be changed.
   What do you want to have happen here?
   Does this problem affect the group?
   What net result do you want after you have taken action?

   Get group agreement.

4. Get Facts.

   Steward first, as he recalls them offhand.
   Review subheads with steward—USE CARDS.
   Get additional facts from group—USE CARDS.

5. Weigh and Decide.

   Fit facts—Look for gaps and contradictions with group.
   Possible Action:
   What facts used?—From steward.
   Check practices and policies with steward.
   Check objective first with group, then last with steward.
   Check probable effect on individual, group, union, and production, with steward.

6. Balance of Case.

   Facts used (from steward).

7. Check Step 3.

   Subheads—with steward.
   Why?—How?—Timing?

8. Check Step 4.

   Subheads—with steward.
   When?—How often?—What?

9. Check Objective.

   Steward.

10. Foundations (if applicable)

    Steward.

(Thank steward and clear board except questions and steps.)

TAKING PREVENTIVE ACTION AND CHECKING RESULTS

Before session starts, place on board:	Just what is this Local Union President trying to accomplish?	1. Get the Facts 2. Weigh and Decide 3. Take Action 4. Check Results

---

Time Table
Allow
30 min

PRACTICE ON STEPS 3 AND 4

1. Make appropriate opening comments.

2. By the use of the Tom problem in Session II we discussed securing the facts through getting personal opinions and feelings.

Using the problem about the old hand in our last session we practiced on Step 2, Weigh and Decide. In this session we are going to hit hard on Steps 3 and 4, "Take Action," and "Check Results."

Underline Steps 3 and 4.	**3. Take Action** **4. Check Results**

Now I an going to present a problem which shows how a local union president took action which was preventive, and how he checked the results of that action.

3. Because of expansion, scarcity of labor, and many other reasons, changes are taking place in organizations throughout the country.

There are many different types of changes such as:

      change in shift
      change in arrangement of benches or machines

This problem illustrates ONE KIND of change.

4. Tell the opening of the problem of the woman supervisor.

The plant superintendent called Bob Jones, the local union president, into his office and told him that the management had decided to use women supervisors as well as men. The superintendent told Bob that he was going to fill supervisory vacancies with women on the basis of seniority and ability, as was the rule with men.

He also told him that both men and women supervisors were to have the same authority and the same opportunity for advancement. Bob considered this very carefully and reviewed the following facts.

One supervisory position had to be filled, and no qualified men were available. All men capable of supervisory responsibility had been upgraded or had been taken into the armed forces. Most of the new employees who had come to the plant in the last 18 months were women.

Bob was informed that a well qualified woman had been selected for the job. As she was to be the first woman supervisor in the plant, Bob anticipated trouble. This was a major change. It looked probable that both men and women members might not like having a woman in authority. More women supervisors would probably be appointed later.

This was the problem Bob faced.

Should he do anything about it?

5. Discuss how this problem came up—saw it coming.

6. Obtain objective—use standard procedure.

Get from group and place on board:

To get woman supervisor accepted

7. Go through Step 1—Get Facts—Use standard procedure.

Get facts from group – list on board, but not necessarily in this order.

Facts

No women supervisors before
Rule – seniority — ability
Same authority and opportunity
One job open
No qualified men
Woman selected
Anticipated trouble

Review the subheads Step 1—Use standard procedure.

8. Go through Step 2—use standard procedure.

Weigh and decide

Possible Actions

List possible actions
which group suggests.
They may be:

Mass meeting
Notice on bulletin board
Say nothing

_____

_____

_____

9. Check all possible actions against objective, and probable effect on individual, group, union, and production.

Bob thought the situation over pretty carefully. Then he talked individually with his fellow union officers and also he talked individually to those of the members who were looked on as natural leaders. He gave them the facts and asked for their help.

There was quite a commotion—some members said they wouldn't stand for it. Bob gave them a chance to do their talking and blowing off. Eventually the workers agreed.

By the time the new supervisor took over her work the outburst was over and the members cooperated in accepting her. Before she went into her department Bob talked with her. He told her that since she was going to be the first woman supervisor in the plant she might run into some difficulty and that she must not be easily offended. He asked her to do her best because it would not only affect her but also other women members of the union who would be appointed as supervisors later.

During the first day on her new job, Bob talked with his fellow union officers and later in the day with the natural leaders he had talked with before. They informed him that apparently the new supervisor was accepted and everything was O.K. Bob, to be sure that his preventive action was effective, kept in close touch with the situation for some time.

11. Get union president's action from group and list on board:

ACTION

Gave the facts in advance
    to fellow officers —
    natural leaders
Asked their help
Let them blow off steam
Asked cooperation of
    new supervisor

What facts did Bob consider?

12. Discuss Step 3, TAKE ACTION—Standard Procedure—
Use cards. Get from group or make the following points
yourself:

Bob handled this himself—why?

> Bob felt it was his job as local union president, and he
> was best qualified to handle it.

Did Bob get help? What advantage was it?

> Bob got help from fellow officers and natural leaders be-
> cause they were in a position to help him get acceptance
> of the change.

Should Bob have referred this to his district office?

> Bob felt he should handle it.

In what way did Bob's timing contribute to the success of his
action?

> Bob allowed just the right time for them to blow off steam
> and cool off before the woman supervisor took over.

Could Bob have passed the buck? HOW?

> Could have blamed management for a bad idea.

13. Discuss Step 4, CHECK RESULTS—standard procedure.
Use cards.

How soon? Why was it important for Bob to check immediately?

> This change affected the whole plant.

How often? Bob kept in close touch with the situation. Why?

> Bob must check closely until he is certain the change is
> accepted.

Did Bob check effect upon attitudes, relationships, and output?
What did he look for?

> Good attitude of fellow officers indicates acceptance of
> change. Good relationship with members in her depart-
> ment proves her acceptance.

Did Bob accomplish his objective? How did he know? He used
Step 4.

14. What foundation points were used in this problem?

Bring out Foundations 3 and 4:

"Tell people in advance about changes that will affect them."

"Make best use of each person's ability."

Clear the board except question and steps.

DISCUSS EFFECT OF CHANGE

Let's take a look at the importance of preparing for the introduction of changes which affect individuals and groups.

Making that change in Bob's department was something new. Members had personal feelings about how this change would affect them.

People generally get used to doing things in a particular place or in a certain way. We are all inclined to question whether it is necessary to change the things we have become accustomed to.

Do workers resist changes which affect their work place or tools or the people they will be working with or next to?

This, then, is a place where one of our foundations for good Union Job Relations comes in—tell members in advance about changes that will affect them.

Preparing the way for a change is surely an equally good thing to do when changes in payment plans, hours, location of the department, new machinery, new products or material are about to be introduced. The same applies to all changes in union policy or rules.

The first boy put into a group of oldtimers, or a woman on machines that have always been run by men, are typical of problems stewards can do something about in advance.

Preparation of this sort prevents problems from arising later, saves time, and improves relationships.

But even though the way has been prepared for the change, it still wise to check the results to find out how the individual or the members of the union accommodate themselves to the change.

SUPERVISORS' PROBLEMS

Handle 3 problems
2 problems 30 min. each
1 problem 25 min.
Standard Procedure

Clear the board.

Just what is this local

union president trying

to accomplish?

To get woman supervisor accepted.

Facts

No women supervisors
  before
Rule — seniority — ability
Same authority and
  opportunity
One job open
No qualified men
Woman selected
Anticipated trouble

---

1. Get the Facts
2. Weigh and Decide
3. <u>Take Action</u>
4. Check Results

Weigh and Decide

Possible Actions

  Mass meeting
  Notice on bulletin board
  Say nothing

ACTION

Gave the facts in advance,
  to fellow officers —
  natural leaders
Asked their help
Let them blow off steam
Asked cooperation of
  new supervisor

STANDARD PROCEDURE

1. Ask steward to tell problem.	Head of table. Does this involve you and somebody whom you represent? Have you taken action? Tell up to final action.
2. How problems come up.	Where appropriate, stress; you sensed, or anticipated a change.
3. Get objective.	Get from steward: Something to shoot at. May be changed. What do you want to have happen here? Does this problem affect the group? What net result do you want after you have taken action? Get group agreement.
4. Get Facts.	Steward first, as he recalls them offhand. Review subheads with steward—USE CARDS. Get additional facts from group—USE CARDS.
5. Weigh and Decide.	Fit facts—Look for gaps and contradictions with group. Possible Action: What facts used?—From steward. Check practices and policies with steward. Check objective first with group, then last with steward. Check probable effect on individual, group, union, and production, with steward.
6. Balance of Case.	Facts used (from steward).
7. Check Step 3.	Subheads—with steward. Why?—How?—Timing?
8. Check Step 4.	Subheads—with steward. When?—How often?—What?
9. Check Objective.	Steward.
10. Foundations (if applicable)	Steward.

(Thank steward and clear board except questions and steps.)

A STEWARD'S OTHER RELATIONSHIPS

| Before session starts, place on board: | Just what is this steward trying to accomplish? | 1. Get the Facts
2. Weigh and Decide
3. Take Action
4. Check Results |

Time Table
Allow 50 min

STEWARD'S PROBLEMS

1. Make appropriate opening comments.

50 min to here

2. Handle two problems—25 min. each.

Allow 25 min

1. 25 minutes is allowed here if necessary for the handling of the tenth steward's problem, or an additional problem from the group. If this time is not needed, go right on with session.

50 min or 1 hr 15 min to here

THANK GROUP FOR INTEREST AND PARTICIPATION.

Clear board.

Allow 10 min

REVIEW OF JOB RELATIONS CARD

1. Are there any questions about the 4-step method for handling a steward's problem?

2. Review foundations for good relations briefly.

All people like to be treated in accord with foundations of good relations. We all can do something about these things. Putting these foundations to work on the job, day by day, will prevent many problems from developing.

Refer to problem sheet.

3. However, when problems do come up, we have a 4-step method to help us handle these problems.

This method will help you get better results but only if you USE it!

4. Review 4-step method including subheads, briefly.

5. Review tips for getting personal opinions and feelings. Try to get as many as possible from group.

Put on board:

How to get opinions and feelings

Don't argue
Encourage individuals to talk
about what is important to
them
Don't interrupt
Don't jump to conclusions
Don't do all the talking yourself
Listen

6. Considering the importance of people in the situation and knowing what is important to the individual person is not a matter of right or wrong or just or unjust. It is simply a common-sense approach to good stewardship.

This is one of the hardest parts of the steward's job—it may be thought to take too much time, but day-by-day use of this skill of dealing with people will save time in the long run.

The steward who knows his people well enough to build them into a smooth operating group is making his important contribution to war production.

Clear the board.

CLINCH ACCEPTANCE OF THE METHOD

by showing advantages to each steward

1. What do you think *you* will gain from using this method? How will it help you personally in your department?

Without too much insistence, bring out through discussion and place on board such points as:

More confidence in ability
to handle people
Better standing with those
you represent
Better standing with superiors
Fewer headaches
Less criticism
Organized plan to follow

If necessary, use these questions:

Will this help you to handle some problems yourself— instead of passing them on to a staff representative?

If you get the whole story before you make decisions, do you think it will improve relationships in your department?

Will it help to have a regular method to follow? How?

Clear the board.

DISCUSS STEWARD'S OTHER RELATIONSHIPS

Show how he is linked to fellow stewards, to committeemen, to union officers, and to plant management.

1. Quickly re-develop the "Steward's Responsibilities" chart from Session I.

Let's go back to the chart we developed in the first session.

Develop on board
the following
stewardship chart:

So far we have
been looking at
the steward's
relations with
people whose
work he directs.

Is this the only kind
of relationships you
have?

What other people
in the plant do you
work with?

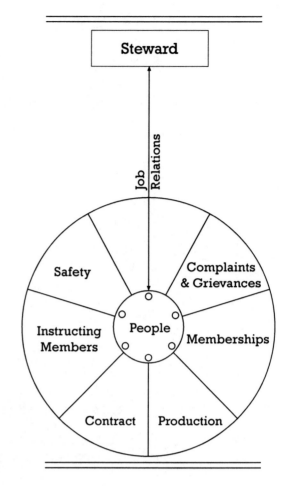

Ask these questions if necessary:

Who gives you your instructions?

Where do your reports go?

What other people do you call on for help?

Do you work with any management representatives?
These management representatives work with people
too.

Add names, boxes, and Job Relations lines.

Each time a Job Relations line is placed on the board, be sure to touch on the fact that this relationship also goes both ways as indicated by the arrowheads.

Also ask "Is this relationship important to the steward?' and "Is this relationship important to the whole union?"
The answer in both cases is "Yes."

Then ask "What can he use to assist him in maintaining this strong relationship?" The answer, of course, is "The foundations and 4-step method. This should be brought out from the group.

The completed chart will appear like this:

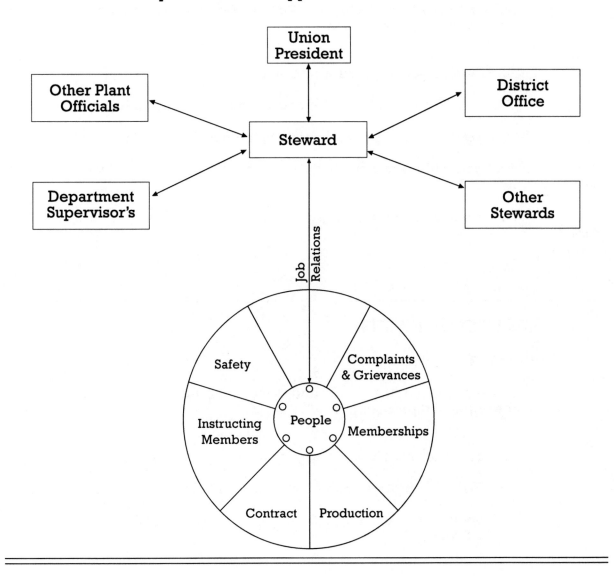

The steward is in touch with all these people and departments.

2. We have said that <u>the steward gets results through people</u>.

Everything you do as a steward depends on people.

How you get along with people is a measure of your standing.

Do the union officers think it's an asset for a steward to have the reputation of working well with people?

With all these people, it will be a good idea to remember, first of all, that they are all people and must be treated as individuals.

And we must realize that there is a Job Relations line between the steward and all these other people on the chart—and if we are to keep good relations with them we must use these foundation points.

Before you take any action—before you go to another union officer or to a steward—you'll want to make certain you've got the facts.

And be sure you have the whole story.

That you "Weigh and Decide" and not jump to conclusions.

That you "Take Action" and not pass the buck.

And you will always come to this final test when you "Check Results."

Did you action strengthen Union Job Relations?

> Leave chart on board.

CREATE CONVICTION

that each will use this skill

1. Maybe sometimes you wonder whether what *you* do helps the union and production.

2. > Ask each man how many people he represents <u>directly</u>.
    >
    > Write the figures on the blackboard, beside the chart.
    >
    > Total them—put the figure in center of chart ABOVE "<u>People</u>."

That many people <u>do</u> influence war production.

And what <u>you</u> do, influences those people.

3. ⌐ Emphasize the strategic position of the steward. ⌐

Everyday relationships count.

★ 4. We are all working on the same job—turning out war
★ production for the men in the armed forces.

★ We all have one customer—Uncle Sam.

★ One objective—to win the war.

⌐ END HERE NO MATTER HOW EARLY ⌐

_____

⌐ Clear the board as members of group are leaving. ⌐

STANDARD PROCEDURE

1. Ask steward to tell problem.

Head of table. Does this involve you and somebody whom you represent? Have you taken action? Tell up to final action.

2. How problems come up.

Where appropriate, stress; you sensed, or anticipated a change.

3. Get objective.

Get from steward:
Something to shoot at. May be changed.
What do you want to have happen here?
Does this problem affect the group?
What net result do you want after you have taken action?

Get group agreement.

4. Get Facts.

Steward first, as he recalls them offhand.
Review subheads with steward—USE CARDS.
Get additional facts from group—USE CARDS.

5. Weigh and Decide.

Fit facts—Look for gaps and contradictions with group.
Possible Action:
What facts used?—From steward.
Check practices and policies with steward.
Check objective first with group, then last with steward.
Check probable effect on individual, group, union, snd production, with steward.

6. Balance of Case.

Facts used (from steward).

7. Check Step 3.

Subheads—with steward.
Why?—How?—Timing?

8. Check Step 4.

Subheads—with steward.
When?—How often?—What?

9. Check Objective.

Steward.

10. Foundations (if applicable)

Steward.

(Thank steward and clear board except questions and steps.)

Union Job Relations Reference 1

UNION JOB RELATIONS IN THE FIELD

The following policies and procedures, which are concerned chiefly with quality control of Union Job Relations, are stated for the Union Job Relations Trainer's guidance and information.

1. Union Job Relations is to be put on exactly as outlined in the manual.

2. During the first 10-hour program put on by any Union Job Relations Trainer, he will be visited by an Institute Conductor or a Quality Control man for at least one session and preferably two.

3. Each Union Job Relations Trainer may be visited in sessions regularly thereafter once a month.

4. No Union Job Relations Trainer shall remain on the active list unless he puts on at least one 10-hour program in 90 days.

5. All Union Job Relations Trainers are expected to attend coaching sessions at the request of the T.W.I. District Office.

6. Union Job Relations sessions shall be limited to groups of 10 stewards.

7. In order to be certified, participants must attend all five sessions in their logical sequence, participate satisfactorily, and present a problem.

8. For certification purposes, we will count the steward who brings an unsolved problem and, as it is being handled, decides he does not have all the facts, thereby shutting off further handling of the problem, because there is evidence that this person does understand the basic step of Job Relations. It is, of course, best to have him present the rest of the facts at a later session.

Union Job Relations Reference 2

TIPS FOR TRAINERS

Opening the Sessions

Have conference room ready and be there <u>ahead</u> of scheduled time—if you start <u>on time</u>, the group will make an extra effort to be prompt.

Urge some top union officer to introduce you to each group. His appearance and endorsement of the program is important.

The 10-hour sessions of Union Job Relations are held so that stewards will learn and practice the 4 steps and the application of the foundations. These sessions are not for the purpose of entertainment or morale building. Beware of "interesting" sessions.

Start at once and continue to emphasize that what we are doing is getting practice in the use of the method. In this practice we arrive at possible actions but they are not to be construed as decisions. We, in analyzing and applying the procedure, are not as close to the problem as the steward who actually must make the decision. We can definitely obtain experience in the use of the method by applying the method to another's problem, but generally, any possible actions arrived at are not as reliable as those that are obtained through the use of the method by the steward who must actually make the decisions.

Avoid a classroom atmosphere and above all do not be an expert. You are not running a one-man personnel relations bureau.

Don't take too much time to give your own experience and background. Your purpose is to set a pattern for the members to use in introducing themselves.

Stress on Method

Remember to follow and use the card. See that the members of the group follow and use the card in all discussions.

Constantly check yourself to see that you are not laying too much stress on something which particularly appeals to you at the expense of other points.

Show your enthusiasm for this program. Enthusiasm is contagious. After several groups, Union Job Relations may become an old story to you. Remember you are setting the standard for the group. The program can be no better than the trainer. Continue to be thorough at all times. A sloppy job by a trainer usually does more harm than good.

Bring out to the group the reasons for throwing the problems against the plan— to give them practice in using it. We are trying to acquire a skill. Your job during the ten hours is to sell the plan to all ten stewards and give them basic training in its use.

Don't just read from the Manual—talk informally with feeling and expression. Make it live! Don't lecture or preach.

Working with the Group

Don't direct your remarks and questions to a favored few—get all members to participate.

Practice good relations with your groups. Don't argue—winning an argument may not convince the other fellow.

Don't try to imitate the personality of your Institute Conductor. Put your own personality into your performance, but stick to the ideas and thoughts outlined in the manual.

Don't put yourself on a pedestal above the group. Be one of them. You will earn their respect if you do a good job putting on the sessions as outlined in the manual.

Be alert when a member gives you an answer even when you are doing something else. Remember it and come back to him. Be constantly on the watch for contributions from individuals in the group. Allow them to express their views and don't try to rearrange or distort their contributions to suit some thought or idea you have in mind.

Be constantly on the lookout for background material contributed by the group with reference to the foundations. If necessary, ask members if they know of any instances where the foundations, if applied, would have prevented a problem from arising.

In an office group, particularly, stewards should be told that they do not need to take notes and they should be specifically directed <u>not</u> to take notes on other stewards' problems.

Handling Stewards' Problems

Reference 3, "Standard Procedure for Handling a Steward's Problem," is the final authority. (For the convenience of the trainer, a condensed form appears at the end of each session.) The steps in the procedure are to be followed <u>exactly</u>. They are designed to give the individual steward more practice. Be sure to get recognition of how the problem came up and the importance of preventive action. It is important to establish a real objective—see that the steward does not look just at the handling of the problem, but at the overall effect or results he wishes.

Avoid constant use of the same objectives repeatedly in all stewards' problems. Vary them and make appropriate to the problem. Help the steward reason out his objective but don't dominate his thinking.

Make "Fact" statements short and to the point.

Remember that all check-points in Step 2 are to be used. The objective, because it is used first, is no more important than the rest of the points.

When someone suggests a broad possible action like "get him interested" ask a "how" question in order to bring the possible action down to something more specific. Otherwise possible actions are ambiguous when we test against the objective.

If a steward claims he doesn't make decisions, point out that a recommendation is a decision. If a steward has a record of making good recommendations, then any that he makes are apt to be considered seriously by his superiors.

Don't let the group give you just any possible action. We want real thinking here. Use "What would you do based on these facts if this problem were dumped into your lap?"

Be sure the members of the group understand that they are not being led to a decision. Decisions cannot be made in a conference room. We are never sure we have <u>all</u> the facts and we do not know the individuals concerned.

Again, the fact that nothing is done is often a decision. When a problem arises the steward sometimes decides not to take any action, or that he should report the matter to his superiors. The fact that he decided to do nothing himself may be an important decision.

When a member of the group asks you a question pertinent to the steward's problem, refer it to the steward instead of trying to answer it yourself.

Don't indicate by your words or actions which possible action you think should be used. A trainer's function is to guide the thinking of the steward and the group through our various steps. We are not making a decision for the steward, but drilling on a method which each steward can use to arrive at his own decision on what action he should take. The steward should know the probable effect of any action on his objective, the individual, the group, the union, and production, better than the trainer or any other member of the group.

Neither you nor the group is "solving" the steward's problem. We are developing our skill in using the foundations and the 4-step method. This is the tool that the steward can use to solve his own problems.

Don't expert (express personal opinions) by saying, "I think." Questions tempting you to do so should be redirected to the members of the group. A good trainer gets the group to do most of the thinking according to the pattern set by the manual. Job Relations is designed to get stewards to think and reason according to a pattern as a basis for sound actions or as an aid to sound action.

Blackboard Work

Don't obstruct the view of the blackboard when discussing blackboard work.

Keep these three things in mind when at the board:

1. Write legibly.
2. Stand at the side of your work as much as possible.
3. Talk while writing.

Do not change the steward's own words unless necessary to avoid highbrow phrasing. However, facts should be briefed on the board. Try, whenever possible, to get the sense and the meaning of the facts in from three to five words. Then check to make sure of meaning, but avoid highbrow phrasing. If someone gives AS A FACT "emotional instability" or "social maladjustment" make it specific. The facts—not their interpretation—are to be put on the board. Ask the steward to tell you what instances make him, say that, and put on the board some specific thing like "had hysterics in office."

Make all blackboard work neat and readable. Talk or ask questions while at the blackboard in order to hold the groups attention.

Describing Practice

In the last fifteen minutes of Session I spend some time enlarging on the procedure that will be followed in handling problems; explain that each steward will come to the head of the table and simply state the facts of the case. The trainer will place them on the board and the group will get experience in using the 4-step method. Emphasize that no comments or criticism will be made. It is important that the stewards realize that they will not be criticized.

Emphasize at the end of Sessions II, III, and IV that to receive a certificate each steward must present a problem. Now that they know what the problems actually are, the regulations about certification mean something.

If people present problems which do not involve the direct relationship with someone represented, the objective is apt to turn out to be of the "either or" or "whether or not" variety. The method applies in horizontal relationships, but for group practice we want to have a real objective to shoot at and therefore we want direct relationships.

If stewards say they have no problems and if they really are stewards, ask them whether they have been doing some preventive work to keep problems from arising. This is particularly useful during Session IV when the Trainer's problem has illustrated how a steward used both the foundations and the 4-step method to keep department conditions smooth and prevent problems from arising.

The Manual

A typographical code has been used to show whether material is:

- to be quoted
- to be presented in trainer's own words
- to be put on the board
- a direction to the Trainer

This code immediately precedes Session I (p. xxi).

Follow the suggested timing for each section. Experience has shown that the time indicated is needed to get the point over. If a particular section takes longer or shorter time than is indicated in the manual, then the timing gives you some idea as to how much you are ahead or behind.

Start each session on time and close on time.

After each session you conduct, go over the manual and the problem handling to check yourself on omissions or failures to get a particular point over to the group. Keep studying your manual, including the references. The Institute only gave you a start. Familiarity with the content of the manual will improve your confidence and effectiveness as a trainer. If you are not sure of your interpretation of any section of the manual, check with the Job Relations men in the T.W.I. District Office.

Be very careful that any remarks you make supplementing the manual pertain to a particular paragraph in the manual. In other words, thoroughly analyze each paragraph or sentence, being sure you know what the meaning is. It is a common fault for trainers, in trying to supplement the manual, to be sidetracked and then have difficulty in getting back on the beam.

"Following the manual" does not mean sitting down and reading it. Learn it— then check yourself, constantly. When there is board work to do, push your chair under the table and stay on your feet. Lean on the back of your chair to look at the manual but do not go back to your seat during the chart work in Sessions I and V, or during the blackboard work on a problem.

Follow your Manual. Omissions, overemphasis, or foreign material may lead you into trouble. Do not mark up the manual. Follow it exactly.

Job Relations Reference 3

STANDARD PROCEDURE FOR HANDLING A
SUPERVISOR'S PROBLEM

---

1. Ask steward to come to head of table and stay there until the problem handling is completed.

Ask steward—"Does this problem involve you and somebody you represent?"

(Under no circumstances permit the steward to use a hypothetical problem, or one in which he was not involved as a steward.)

Say—"Have you taken action on your problem?"

If the answer is "Yes," have him tell his problem up to—but not including—final action.

To keep him from telling what the final action was, make a simple statement as to the reason for stopping. The purpose is to get better group participation—yet to give the steward the full benefit of his practice problem. Inform the steward that he is to tell the group about the incident or situation that made him realize he had a problem on which he had to take action, plus any fact-getting steps he then went through, but to stop before he gives any interpretation of the facts or mentions any decisions or actions.

Under no circumstances, interrupt the man, even to keep him from telling the final action. If he generalizes, let him alone (unless the problem is very long) but when he finishes make some such remark as "you say this is always happening—let's take just one instance." In problems involving large numbers of people, try to reduce the problem to what involves only one person.

2. After he tells his problem, ask the steward in which one of the four ways this problem came to his attention (or comment on it, yourself).

a. You sensed a change in your department.

(EXAMPLE: Found changed relation or break in usual set-up.)

b. You anticipated a change in your department.

(EXAMPLE: You know a change is coming and want to prepare for it.)

c. This one came to you.

(EXAMPLE: An individual made a request or protested.)

d. You ran into this one.

(EXAMPLE: It just happened.)

The examples stated under a, b, c, and d above are to be used only as necessary. Should the steward question what is meant, the purpose of bringing out how problems arise is to make stewards more aware of the preventive work that may be done, particularly in regards to *a* and *b*.

STRESS *a* and *b* at every opportunity, pointing out that they are in the preventive areas. To vary this procedure after handling several stewards' problems, you might ask any one of the group for the four ways that problems arise.

3. Ask steward: "Just what are <u>you</u> trying to accomplish?"

(Do not erase this question when clearing the board at the conclusion of the first supervisor's problem. It will speed up your work if you do not have to rewrite it.)

The objective is something to shoot at. It may be difficult to determine. It may have to be changed in the course of handling the problem.

<u>Help</u> the steward to state his objective—but do not force him to accept someone else's statement. Question the objective if it seems short-sighted or mistaken.

Use of the following questions will be helpful:

What makes this a problem?

What do you want to have happen here?

What effect is this having on production? On the union?

Are any other people in the department concerned?

What results do you want to get out of this?

If the steward gives as his objective one that appears to be inadequate, such as "to get the old hand off his neck," help him to get a long-range view by asking "why" in order to get him to see that the accomplishment he wants in the end is "to eliminate trouble in the group."

Get agreement from group that the steward has chosen exactly what he is trying to accomplish. The following questions may be helpful:

Do you see exactly what he is aiming at?

Do you "get" the objective?

Would you have the same one?

What would you have in mind?

Do not write the objective given by the group on the board unless the steward is in agreement. The purpose of asking the other stewards to participate is to get them thinking and give the steward telling the problem the benefit of their thoughts.

4. Ask the steward for important facts and list them on the board as given by him. Do not number the facts. (Your board work should be brief but accurate. Write his statements in three or four words.)

Do not let this board work DRAG. Help the steward recall facts he has already mentioned. Putting down the facts is not a memory exercise. Suggest them. However, he is the referee—do not change or interpret his facts.

USE THE CARD FROM HERE ON OUT

Say—Let us look at our cards.

Make sure that everybody in the group is looking at his card before proceeding. Direct the questions to the steward.

> Ask—Have we reviewed the record and do we have those facts on the board? Do not let this go on a "yes" or "no" answer.

> Go through each sub-head in the same manner. Find out what facts were obtained by talking with the individual to get opinions and feelings. Show them on the board. Apply the "Tips for getting opinions and feelings" if appropriate. Ask why the worker did what he did.

This procedure may help get additional important facts and may preclude "talk with him" as a possible action in Step 2. Put additional facts, supplied in answer to group's questions, on board. Do not separate them from the previously listed facts by a dotted line or space.

> Ask the steward: Are these all the facts needed for a decision?

If the steward who is presenting the problem says he does not have all the facts and if he has not yet taken action, the steps that will be taken to get more facts may be discussed. They will not be put on the board and there will be no discussion of possible actions or any other part of Step 2.

If the steward who is presenting the problem says he has already taken action, and during the discussion says that he did not have all the facts, handling of the problem continues.

> Ask the steward: Do you want the group to pitch in now?

> Ask group: Do you want to ask the steward any questions about this problem?

> Ask group: If you were in the position of this steward, would you want any additional facts?

If facts that seem trivial are suggested, you may want to ask the steward:

> Is that fact underline important in helping us to come to a decision in this problem?

By doing this, many times the steward will wash out irrelevant facts. At this time you can, as part of the group, ask questions about the problem, but do not do this if group is working readily on these points.

All of the following information will probably not be needed in any one problem, but the Trainer may need to ask the following "smoke-out questions" in the vein of, do you need to know —, would it make any difference if—?

Employee's job—just what he does

Time on present job and length of service with company

Work and training background before coming on with company

Present working environment

Work record: production, quality, housekeeping, absence, etc.

What (if any) recent changes have been made in the working conditions of the department which may affect the problem?

What is the working relationship between employee and foreman, from the employee's point of view?

Job rating of employee—how is he getting along?

Wage rate of employee—any recent change?

What (if any) union and company policies are involved?

Personal data concerning the employee

    a. Age
    b. Marital status and home life
    c. Outside activities: hobbies, social life, etc.

Personality, temperament, attitude of employee

What persons other than employees are involved?

What intermediate action (if any) has been taken in the problem? (This does not refer to a final solution.)

If a member of a group says, "But suppose it had been this way"—remind them that we deal only with facts. The Trainer must be particularly careful not to say "Let's assume" or "Suppose it had been."

Then ask — Are we reasonably sure we have the whole story?

If any member of the group says that he does not think there are enough facts, it is appropriate to ask him what part of the card brings him to that conclusion. The trainer may summarize by saying, "Then, if you were in the steward's shoes, you would feel you did not have the whole story and you would not be ready to decide on your action until you had more facts." This applies whether the steward presenting the problem has taken action or not.

5. Say—Let's take a look at the second step, Weigh and Decide. Write on board—*WEIGH AND DECIDE*. Here is where we think about these facts.

Quote the card —

The card says fit the facts together.

In fitting the facts together, let us see first if there are any contradictions; second, if there are any gaps that call for additional facts. <u>Discuss</u> these points.

Consider their bearing on each other. Do not make this either a statement or a "yes" or "no" question. This is part of the method.

Do the facts indicate some possible actions?

After this, again quote the card —

What possible actions are there? Write on board, under <u>Weigh and Decide</u>—Possible Actions.

Explain that you are asking the group to suggest "Possible Actions" in order to:

get practice in Weighing and Deciding

show that there usually are several "Possible Actions"

You are <u>not</u> trying to make the decision for the steward, or criticize what he has already done.

Select one member of the group and ask: What would <u>you</u> do if <u>you</u> had <u>this</u> problem?

Ask him what facts he used. Do not let them be referred to as the "first and third"—name them. These are the facts which bear on each other and which produced the "Possible Action."

Ask the steward whether the action is possible within his company's policies and practices. If he says yes, write the "Possible Action" on the board.

Repeat with two more stewards in the group.

A steward who points out in the discussion of Step 1 that he believes all the facts have not been obtained should not be asked for a possible action.

If anyone gives as a possible action such suggestions as "get the facts" or "find out why," it is handled by saying, "You mean you would want to get more facts before you decided on what you would do to handle this problem. Any steward must feel personally sure that he has the facts before he considers action—that is the meat of this Job Relations program. But at this point we will let the stewards who feel there <u>are</u> enough facts, suggest the actions *they* would consider." When such a possible action as "Talk with the worker" is suggested, clarify the meaning. If it is "to find out," then it is not a possible action. If it is "to persuade him," re-phrase it before writing on the board. Get agreement to write it as "reason," "convince," or "persuade" and ask how he would do it to make it specific.

If additional facts are brought out at any time, write them on the board. After there are three or four "Possible Actions" on the board, check the first one by:

Asking the group whether this will accomplish the objective of:

Asking the steward about the objective, briefly—yes or no

Asking the steward about the probable effect on:

the individual
the group
the union
production

Do not cross off Possible Actions even if the discussion proves them unwise. Crossing off may indicate to some the making of a decision by vote.

Remind the group that skill in Weighing and Deciding can be learned through practice. You become familiar with areas to explore, and what to be on the lookout for (but don't jump to conclusions).

If, in the discussion, there is some such statement made as "All these people coming from farms (or from stores, or all women, or any other generalization) are no good," or "All the fellows about to be called in the draft are hard to handle," the trainer must not let it stand. Point out that individuals are different, and that you can make a bad decision if you jump to conclusions about what they are like.

6. Have the stewards state balance of his problem if action has been taken. Write it on the board. Make no comment on the action taken. Ask steward what facts he used in selecting this action. If action has not been taken, proceed to Steps 3 and 4. Your lead-in can be, "When you take action on this problem, are you going to handle this yourself, etc.—."

7. Check sub-heads under Step 3 with steward. Ask "Why" and "How" after sub-heads when pertinent. Get brief group discussion on timing the interval between reaching a decision and taking action. Ask group in every problem—"Let us look at our cards."

New stewards are often concerned about being "by-passed." Remind them that they are by-passed when they fail to size up situations effectively in order to take the right action—the action that solves a problem.

Some stewards feel they have no responsibility in connection with people whom they represent because the union headquarters takes care of dues and a special committee handles grievances. But in all problems, the man closest to the individual member does have a relationship with that person—he must make it good in order to get the most out of production. It will strengthen his leadership when he does. With new stewards, particularly, there will be many requests for help on "What do I do when he says he won't do what I ask him to, or else shows that he doesn't want to?" Handle this in terms of the particular person involved. There aren't any general rules, and the steward has to stop looking for them. This is a real situation, and the only help anyone else can give him is to tell him to look at the whole situation—the persons involved, including himself, and the effect on other people—try it and see how it works.

If a steward asks: "What do you think of what I did?" it will be helpful to say, "Well, let's take a look at what you were trying to accomplish. What were the results?"

Do not lose any chances to emphasize to the stewards in your group that it is a definite part of the steward's job to realize just exactly how far his own responsibility and ability extend in the handling of Job Relations problems.

Remind stewards to always ask themselves: "Is this something I should handle myself? Do I need help? Is this something I must pass on?"

Some cases will be brought in which involve people heading toward being fired, and sometimes that is the answer. Look at the effect on other people.

Is the effectiveness of the person more than the trouble he causes? In these days, we must keep everyone we can, if he is useful, but there are still some people who have to be fired.

8. Check sub-heads under Step 4 with supervisor. Use "when," "how often," and "what" after sub-heads when pertinent.

Ask how the steward can check results, and what he will look for.

9. Have the steward check whether or not objectives were accomplished or whether they may be accomplished if the problem has not reached final action. Let him tell "why."

10. Say, "Let's look at the other side of our card." (Make sure that they are looking at the cards.) Use the foundations in a preventive sense. Ask the steward, "Do any of our foundations for good relations apply in this problem?" "Could the use of any foundations have prevented this problem?"

Consider: "People must be treated as individuals."

If you are convinced that nothing on the foundation side applies, omit this step.

Thank the steward for contributing a problem. (Do not comment or pass judgment on actions or results.)

Union Job Relations Reference 4

A WAY OF LOOKING AT THE STEWARD'S JOB

In working with stewards it is important to remember that their chief importance is as representatives. Just as the supervisor represents management, the steward represents and acts for union members.

For the most part the line and staff organizations of management and of labor are parallel, and many of the personnel problems encountered by management representatives are also faced by union officers at corresponding levels.

A production department seldom runs along smoothly without interruption. About the time a group is working together smoothly, changes usually occur. Whether these changes are in the form of expanding schedules, improvements in methods, shifts in organization, or new employees, they always create problems.

Stewards need to know not only the contract and the procedures of their union, but the individual members as well. Expert knowledge of union regulations is not sufficient to make a good steward. The steward needs to give attention to the particular characteristics of each individual for no two of them have exactly the same experience, abilities, and desires.

The steward will not always find it possible to apply these particular practices to his own situation, since they were used in different situations. But if he will look for the general ideas which the other fellows' practices illustrate, he will find that they can be applied to his problems too. These ideas have been derived from the experience of men in the shop.

It must be remembered that to the worker, a job means more than just a pay check every week or doing mechanical operations over and over between in-and-out whistles. It means that he is part of an organization, wherein he has a particular place. It means that he is a human being who wonders what kind of people his fellow-workers are, what they are going to expect of him, how he should approach his steward, etc. Representing a union member includes helping the worker to adjust himself to his surroundings, giving him an idea of the union of which he is part, and the particular role he is to fill in it.

This is the point of view from which we approach these five sessions.

The steward facing hour by hour the difficulties of enforcing a contract may easily overlook the difficulties of his workers. It is natural for him to think most of results and to spend little time on people. Yet there are conditions in each department which prevent the development of wholesome attitudes toward associates and the union.

New stewards can look back and remember a few things—what difficulties did you run into? Try to look at the department situation through the operator's eyes.

Look at the men—their minds, muscles, feelings, and attitudes. Observe them and talk with them. Notice what they do. Attempt to analyze their actions. Listen to their comments and encourage them to talk because the more clearly you know each operator as a person, the better you can represent him.

Understanding people is not a simple process. The steward who says, "I can size up a man as soon as I meet him," is usually fooling himself. It will be helpful to notice some of the habits which actually hinder us in understanding them.

The "Die-Casting" Habit—Too often, as we observe individuals, we try to sort them into types. To put it another way, we try to force them into imaginary molds which we have set up in our minds, much as the die-caster squirts metal into different kinds of molds. They may be different shapes before they go in, but they're all alike when they come out!

We feel that we have completely cataloged Bill Jones when we say that he is a "good mixer," that we have defined Tom Smith when we put him down as a "tough customer." But we can't do that with people if we really wish to understand them. We must study each one from all sides, not pour them into molds or cast them into types.

The "Just Like" Habit—"He reminds me for all the world of Bill Brown," we say, and thereafter we notice most easily the traits which are like Bill Brown and ignore those which are different. Once we have made up our minds that he is "like Bill Brown," we close our minds to the possibility of his having other characteristics which we may need to know. We stop studying him, with the result that we never discover many of the interests and abilities which are part of him.

The "Go, No-Go" Habit—"I can tell whether a man will make a good union member as soon as I ask him to do one thing for the union," said a steward. "If he listens carefully to what we want and does it exactly as I tell him, he will make a good man. If he tries to 'dope out' his own way of doing it, he seldom makes a good member." This steward, if he really does follow the way of thinking which he described, is classifying all employees into two classes: (1) Those who follow directions to the letter, and (2) those who try to figure out methods of their own. His gauge of men is two-valued, "go" or "no-go." There is no "in-between." He is applying an inspection technique, not an understanding one.

People are seldom "either-or." Studies of individuals show that approximately two-thirds of them have each of the commonly observed traits to a moderate degree. That is, they are close to the average, and that only a small percentage have markedly large or small degrees of any trait. Not "either-or" but "the degree to which" should be the guiding concept in studying people.

Similarly it is easy to fall into the habit of judging employees solely by how well they do that particular phase of union work in which the steward is most interested, overlooking their participation or lack of participation in other important union activities. People's reactions cannot be measured fairly with any single gauge. They are too complex.

The "Formula" Habit—Closely related to these "stereotype" ways of looking at people, is the practice of dealing with each "type of person" in a certain set manner. It has been said that the way to "handle" the "oldtimer" is to "let him alone," that the best way to get along with the "chronic kicker" is to "lay down the law."

Of course, these methods work a good deal of the time with many of the people with whom stewards have to deal. Otherwise, they would not be so commonly accepted. But they become a hindrance when they are used as excuses for lumping people together in groups or types and avoiding the responsibility of trying to understand each person as an individual.

In short, people cannot be handled like piece parts or an apparatus. Each is an individual, different from every other. "Stereotyping" them, classifying them, standardizing them, or reducing them to formulas—habits of thinking that work well with inanimate things—often proves to be an actual hindrance in handling people.

The "Standardization" Habit—Stewards may become so accustomed to thinking in terms of standards that they look only for <u>common</u> responses of "the worker" and pay little attention to the <u>special</u> interests, abilities, and peculiarities of individual persons. Yet it is these special characteristics that yield fruitful contacts upon which to base effective stewardship. It is the ways in which a person is different, and especially the ways in which he is superior to the "mine run" of people, which furnish the key to his special interests. He tends to develop strong interests in the fields in which he possesses ability. The steward has the problem of taking each of these unique and different personalities, finding out what he is like and to what he will respond, and fitting him into activities which he will be most effective in the union.

How to Understand the Individual Member

How can the steward understand a person who comes into his department well enough to fit him into the union? He can talk with him, question him, observe him, throw out conversational leads to draw him out, listen to him, and think and listen and think, seeking ever to look behind appearances and first impressions into the background of feelings, sentiments and other reactions, to the experiences which make up the man himself.

Keeping in mind that it is not a question of "either-or" but rather of "thee degree to which," the steward can use the following questions in his study of each individual. In using each question, however, the steward must think constantly, "To what extent does he do this? In what degree is this true or not true of him? How far is this aspect important in this individual? Why does he react the way he does?" Here are the questions:

1. Is he "doing a good job?"

2. Does he fail to understand instructions?

3. Does his attention wander from the job?

4. Is he interested in his job?

5. How does he respond to recognition?

6. Does he stand on his own feet?

7. Does he seem ill-adapted to the job?

8. Does he get along well with the other people in the department?

Each of these questions may now be considered a little further.

1. <u>Is he doing a good job?</u>—Does he miss a part of the instructions when he is given a start on the new job? Most likely he does. Is he therefore stupid or careless? Not at all, he is merely human. The human mind has a perfect mechanism for avoiding overload: It simply ignores. If parts of the situation are wholly unrelated to the individual's past experience, or to his present interest, he "pays no attention to them." If the total situation demanding his attention—for example the new job—is complicated, his eyes and ears first grasp only those aspects which interest him most. If his experience with these is satisfying, he soon explores further and is ready for more instruction. The steward can call to the attention of the supervisor or instructor the points of the job he seized upon at the beginning, as cues to his interests, and the rest of the instruction can be related to these interests. Are you sure that he knows just what you expect of him? Have you over-sold the job and is he let down?

2. <u>Does he fail to understand instructions?</u>—Does he misinterpret them? Does he fail to catch the point of the explanation? Does he seem "a bit thick?" The easy way out is to label such a person "dumb" and thus avoid all responsibility for helping him become an efficient operator. This, however, neither saves the man nor gets the work done, and what is more it is usually unnecessary. Most workers who have passed the employment office are high enough in mental capacity to learn readily the jobs to which they have been assigned. When they fail to understand, it is not from "dumbness" but from <u>narrowness of experience</u>. They are like the city boy who, on his first visit to a farm, tried to get a pail of water by calmly holding up the pump handle, waiting for the water to come. Why shouldn't he? He had seen hydrants with pull-up handles but he had never seen a pump in a well.

The worker who learns slowly because of narrow experience can usually be trained by patient, well-planned instruction and often makes a superior operator. Cues to his background and his interests may be gained by encouraging him to talk about the job, listening to him without interruptions, and giving attention as much to what he takes for granted as to what he actually says. Gaps in his background can be filled by giving him actual experience in the shop.

The worker who misinterprets instructions, and thus makes mistakes, is a similar problem. On account of the narrowness of his experience he fails to understand. Where others might have got meaning, he draws a blank because he doesn't know the "code." Yet he fears to reveal his ignorance. What does he do? He bridges the gap by using his imagination and, whenever he guesses wrong, he makes mistakes. The remedy is to make a connection with his meager experience by finding out as much about it as possible and to win his confidence to the point where he is willing to ask questions. It often helps to have him repeat instructions in his own words: "Now just to be sure I've made it clear, tell me what it is you're going to do."

Care in explaining shop terms will help greatly. One worker tells of his first day in the shop thus: "The boss gave me a big pan of little gadgets and said, 'Take these piece parts over to that bench and "mike" 'em. The "max." and "min." are six and ten.' Then off he went and I spent the next 3 hours trying to figure out what mike, min., and max. had to do with the job, and what I was supposed to do with the pan of gadgets."

Ignorance of shop terms and shop customs is by no means confined to "new" employees fresh from the employment office. Picture an experienced employee newly transferred from a distant department, trying to adjust himself to a new location and learn a wholly new kind of job. During his years on the old job he has gone along, paying little attention to other organizations, yet now on the new job he is ashamed to reveal his ignorance. He is grateful to the instructor who will take the trouble to discover the limits of his experience and give him the help he needs.

3. <u>Does his attention wander from the job?</u>—Does he seem to be oversensitive to noises, changes in light and ventilation, presence of other workers or passers-by? If so, he is merely responding naturally—acting "like a human being." Most individuals find it hard <u>not</u> to pay attention to all that is going on around them, especially to noises and people.

The new worker, in addition to mastering his skill, has to become accustomed to a "total situation" which is strange and fascinating. In fact, a part of any skill is an ability to ignore everything except the activity itself—to concentrate one's attention on it. Witness the ability of the champion athlete to forget his gallery and lose himself in the game.

Complete absorption in a task and disregard of surroundings amid the distracting noise and activity of a manufacturing plant is not a natural act. It is an achievement—that is, it can be learned. Fortunately, most workers are able to learn it for themselves in a relatively short time. Sometimes it is possible to help the worker who is unusually sensitive to distraction by placing him in a less exposed location where noises are either more uniform or monotonous, or by transferring him to work which requires a broader spread of attention or which includes dealing with a large number of people.

4. <u>Is he interested in his job?</u>—Does he fail to put forth the effort necessary to learn to do the job well? A man will have an interest in a job if he feels that it is in harmony with his own purposes, that it is "getting him somewhere." If he can identify the job with himself, see its connection with his own life, with his cherished ambition, then he is "interested in the job" in the same sense that a man who buys an interest in a business is "interested in" that business. When this happens there is no trouble about effort.

But often the new worker cannot see any relation between his own plan for the future and the job to which he is assigned. The steward can explain to the worker how upgrading takes place and what avenues of advancement are open to him if he is efficient in each job along the line. Some young workers are victims of the "white-collar" craze; their only idea of advancement is to get out of the shop and into the office, without any clear understanding of the possibilities of either. A steward can often render a real service to such young people by giving them facts regarding the values of shop experience, no matter where later promotions or transfers may lead, and helping them to think over their plans and ambitions in the light of these facts rather than on the basis of family or personal prejudice regarding "overalls" or the "white collar."

Occasionally the steward finds an individual who has "hitched his wagon to a star" far beyond the limits of his capacity, background, and education. He may have to help such a person to get his feet on the ground. On the other hand, some learners in the shop seem to have no definite ambition or plan of action for their lives at all. By talking with them and becoming better acquainted, the instructor may be able to discover such an ambition and help the worker to connect his job with it.

Under war conditions it is a powerful stimulus to show each man what he and the department do for the war effort.

Many stewards make it a point to tell the members how their production will be used: "This goes into an airplane to show the pilot so and so—." "This goes into an instrument panel to show so and so—." "Our union fabricates parts for _____ planes a month."

In a highly specialized factory it is difficult to provide the interest which the old craftsman felt in the product of his hands because it was all his own, from raw material to finished master piece. The modern shop, where the worker can see the whole prod-

82

uct fabricated before his eyes, provides an opportunity to revive this kind of interest. The worker can "see what he is doing" and see that it is worthwhile.

Likewise, a worker has more interest in his machine if he understands how it works, the principles of its operation, what it can do, and just as important, what it cannot do; i.e., the limits of its operation. When the worker knows these things, instead of blindly following the directions of the machine setter or the equipment man, he takes an interest in the machine. Because he feels that he understands it, he comes to identify it with himself, just as he does the job in which he "has an interest." It becomes his machine, and thus a new interest in the job is born.

A more simple key to the worker's interest is some activity which he enjoys doing for its own sake. One supervisor makes a practice of talking with the new worker about his hobbies. He discovers what the worker likes to do and often is able to relate the job to these interests, or to help him transfer to a job he enjoys.

Knowledge of his own progress stimulates the learner's interest. The value of operators' performance records as an incentive, especially when presented in graphic form, was discovered long ago. We like to beat our own record, to see ourselves grow in skill, and most of us like to engage in rivalry with others. Rivalry of output, however, is a form of stimulation which has to be handled wisely, especially during the training period. Progress in learning does not always register in daily output. While learning correctness of "form" and developing the ability to reach quality standards, output may not show a daily increase and the worker should not judge his progress by it. The steward can prevent discouragement and loss of interest by directing his attention to this fact.

Then there is the matter of social approval. Any experienced steward knows the value of recognition as a stimulation of interest in the job. Praise is discussed further in a different connection below.

The effectiveness of all these ways of reaching the worker's interests and relating them to the job lies in the fact that a man reacts as a whole. We sometimes talk of training his muscles or his brain or his hands. We can't. His whole self is being trained by every experience he has. We teach the man, not his hand. When he has mastered a skill, the whole man has it, uses it, and is proud of it. The man himself has ambitions to which the job may or may not be related. The man himself enjoys doing it, or is indifferent to it. The man himself basks in the appreciation of his fellows when they recognize that he has done the job well. Anything which connects with his interests affects all parts of him. His eye brightens, his mind becomes more alert, his hand more sure. Recognition of success in one part of the job reacts to heighten his interest in the job as a whole, and he does the whole job better. Conversely, failure in any part of the job depresses the whole man, his work and his attitude toward the job—unless he regards the failure as a challenge, analyzes it, and learns how to overcome it.

The largest factor with which a steward has to deal is his worker's "interests." This emphasizes again the need for the steward to become well acquainted with his workers as persons, to understand their backgrounds of experience, their hopes and purposes for the future, their bents and special abilities, all in order that he may help them to discover real and lasting connections between themselves and their jobs.

5. How does he respond to recognition?—Does praise stimulate him? How does he take criticism?

A little recognition adds zest to the job and stimulates a man's efforts. This is especially true of the learner, because he feels insecure and uncertain about himself anyhow. Building his confidence is part of the job.

The most tangible form of recognition is, of course, the weekly pay envelope. An increase in his rate is a visible goal. But so many factors over which the steward has no control enter into requests for wage increases that he finds other forms of recognition also necessary. When a steward notices that a new man is doing a good job, or when a supervisor tells him so, he can help the new man by telling him he's doing well.

Praise in the presence of the group is an effective form of recognition, so long as it is fair. It is usually stronger than praise in private but more difficult to give because the members of the group are always making comparisons. Both approval and correction are necessary, but criticism given before the group usually results in confusion or resentment.

The new worker learns more from praise than from censure. The reason is simple. He is blundering about, seeking the right way to do each part of the job. When he happens upon a right way, and the instructor approves it, he knows he has got that part of the job, and seeks to repeat it. At the same time he experiences a glow of satisfaction which spurs him on to master other parts of the job. But suppose he tries a wrong way and is "bawled out?" What has he learned? Simply that one way is wrong. He still does not know a right way and may try many other wrong ones before he finds a right one. Meanwhile he feels discouraged because of the disapproval. Such a moment can be seized to demonstrate again the "right way" to do the operation, though that is beside the point here. It is often necessary to point out mistakes but, even at its best, censure or adverse criticism helps the learner too slowly on his way to skill. Instead, it is better to catch him as often as possible doing the right thing, even by chance, and speed him on his way with a word of appreciation.

6. <u>Does he stand on his own feet?</u>—Does he lean on other people too much, or go to the opposite extreme and act as if he knows it all?

Most new workers are a bit fearful and lacking in confidence, some more and some less. They show it in curious and contradictory ways, as the above questions suggest. A little fear when facing a new situation serves to awaken most persons to greater alertness and effort. They are able to rise to the occasion and soon overcome their fears. They "take things in their stride." Yet there are many individuals who lack emotional balance, who have not learned to take life as it comes, to face reality as adults. It is important, however to remember the caution about "die-casting" people into molds, to notice "the degree to which" the individual lacks emotional balance. Differences in individuals range all the way from the person who adjusts himself to the job situation promptly, stands on his own feet and quietly tackles everything in a matter-of-fact way, to the person who leans on others and expects favors, who covers his fears with over boldness, or who seeks to "make a good impression" instead of concentrating his attention on learning the job.

While the steward cannot go along indefinitely trying to help a maladjusted person "grow up," he can often add to the timid man's confidence by pointing out his successes and, on the other hand, bring a bluffer back to reality by facing him with the demands of the job. He is interested at all times in each operator's reactions to the job and to his fellow-workers, because they are facts which affect his doing the job, his attitude toward it, and toward the union.

7. <u>Does he seem ill-adapted to the job?</u>—In spite of the best efforts of line supervisors and personnel organization, employees are sometimes placed on jobs they cannot do satisfactorily. Two cautions are in order here, however.

First: Do not assume that an employee is a misfit in a job until he has been fully and correctly instructed on that job and has shown that he cannot do it successfully. Many men have been called misfits on jobs they never had a fair chance to learn. Often a slow learner makes an excellent operator. It is a misfortune for him if he has to begin the job under a supervisor or instructor without the patience and willingness to instruct. A steward should not ask that a worker be transferred until he is really sure that he is a misfit.

Second: Do not assume that when a worker is a misfit in one job he is useless. Any supervisor of long experience could tell stories of "misfits" who found other places where they made good. Few misfits are totally unfit.

Get acquainted with the employee, win his confidence, discover what he can do and likes to do, find out his difficulties on the job, and see that he either learns it or gets a fair trial at other jobs for which he is better adapted.

8. <u>Does he get along well with other people in the department?</u>—Sometimes men know how to do their jobs well, and yet they are not effective because they do not get along well with the people with whom they work.

Consider whether any differences in your relationships with the various people are part of the situation.

You may need to re-align the team in order to get a group to work together.

THE STEWARD AND THE SUPERVISOR

No one can deny the importance of good working relations between the union's representatives and management's representatives. Because the steward and the supervisor are in immediate contact with the workers in the shop, they control the basic foundations for industrial peace. The best contract in the world between labor and management becomes a scrap of paper unless it works in the plant. This is the job of both the steward and the supervisor. Due to withdrawals to the armed forces there are many inexperienced stewards. They need help and understanding.

It is well to keep in mind that the steward's job is to represent members, not to act as an impartial arbitrator. By the same token, a supervisor must represent management's interests to the best of his ability. However, if both can negotiate on a factual basis, their mutual problems can then be settled on merits without a loss in prestige by either party. Only through mutual understanding and respect between steward and supervisor can we hope to achieve industrial harmony. Without such harmony we cannot achieve a maximum in war production and cooperation in the reconversion programs.

Today as never before the settlement of grievances within a plant is vitally important. Every unsettled grievance tends to lower working efficiency and thus reduces output. When both stewards and supervisors acquire the skill of working with people and handling problems that involve people, they will settle many complaints as soon as they arise and not lean on the slower process of the grievance machinery where decisions may be delayed for months.

SUMMARY

Good stewardship is not a skill which can be mastered over night—human beings are complex. But it is a skill in which you improve on the job, and one which gives returns to you, your department, your plant, your union, and the war effort.

Publications from Enna

From Enna's new classics by Shigeo Shingo to our books and training packages regarding operational excellence, Enna provides companies with the foundation of knowledge and practical implementation ideas that will ensure your efforts to internalize process improvement. Reach your vision and mission with the expertise within these world-class texts. Call toll-free (866) 249-7348, visit us on the web at www.enna.com to order, or request our free product catalog.

Enjoy the rest of the books in our T.W.I. Training Series:

Job Instruction: Sessions Outline and Materials

Job Instruction, a short, intensive training program, was developed in order to provide skills in leadership to new and experienced supervisors alike. Contained within the Job Instruction book are samples, scenarios, and discussion topics which give you the tools necessary to properly instruct new workers and do away with waste and accidents, as well as cut down the time it takes to get a new worker 'up to speed' on his job.
ISBN 978-1-897363-92-8 | 2009 | $34.99 | Item: **922**

Job Methods: Sessions Outline and Materials

In teaching you the method behind the job and how to properly break down a job into its most fundamental parts, this book aims to teach you how to reduce wasteful behavior and wasteful steps within a job. The training material within provides you with worksheets, forms and sample scenarios to give you practice in scrutinizing and simplifying jobs.
ISBN 978-1-897363-93-5 | 2009 | $34.99 | Item: **923**

Job Relations: Sessions Outline and Materials

Job Relations was developed in order to provide management with a tool whereby supervisors could acquire skills in leadership. Contained within the Job Relations book are sample scenarios, discussion topics and instructional diagrams that relate the supervisor and his subordinates, show the dynamic of such a relationship and provide a way of looking at and dealing with these relationships that will benefit everyone in the company.
ISBN 978-1-897363-94-2 | 2009 | $34.99 | Item: **924**

Union Job Relations: Sessions Outline and Materials

Union Job Relations was developed concurrently with Job Relations in order to provide stewards with a way to acquire skills in leadership within their company and union. Contained within the Union Job Relations book are sample scenarios, discussion topics and instructional diagrams that relate the steward to his union, supervisors and the union members he is responsible for, shows the dynamic of such relationships and provide a way of looking at and dealing with these relationships that will benefit everyone in the company.
ISBN 978-1-897363-95-9 | 2009 | $34.99 | Item: **925**

To Order: Enna Corp., 1602 Carolina Street, Unit B3, Bellingham, WA 98229

Program Development Institute

The Program Development Institute was established in order to train people in setting up and implementing an entire training program within their company. Enclosed are worksheets, examples and practice problems to assist in developing the program as a training coordinator. With this book you will learn how to step back and look at the company as a whole, before implementing training and improvements.
ISBN 978-1-897363-96-6 | 2009 | $34.99 | Item: **926**

Problem Solving Training: Sessions Outline and Materials

The Problem Solving workbook instructs on how to properly Isolate, Breakdown, Question and Solve problems. From detailing just how you know you have a problem to charts and diagrams that will assist you in solving the problem, this book is a must read for anyone who deals with production on a daily basis.
ISBN 978-1-926537-00-9 | 2009 | $34.99 | Item: **927**

Bulletin Series

Based on the simple premise that in order to function there has to be an organized structure that recognizes that ongoing training is an investment that will always pay for itself the T.W.I. Bulletin Series is packed with ideas, concepts, and methods that will produce results. Contained within are bulletins that will assist in selecting supervisors, strengthening management and achieving continuous results.
ISBN 978-1-897363-91-1 | 2008 | $34.99 | Item: **914**

Other Books by Enna

Mistaken Kanbans

Let Mistaken Kanbans be your roadmap to guide you through the steps necessary to implement and successful Kanban System. This book will help you to not only understand the complexities of a Kanban System but gives you the tools necessary, and the guidance through real-life lessons learned, to avoid disastrous consequences related to the improper use of such systems.
ISBN 978-1-926537-10-8 | 2009 | $27.99 | Item: **919**

The Toyota Mindset

From the brilliant mind of a legend in the LEAN manufacturing world comes the reasoning behind the importance of using your intellect, challenging your workers and why continuous improvement is so important. For anyone who wishes to gain insight into how the Toyota Production System came to be or wants to know more about the person behind TPS this book is a must read!
ISBN 978-1-926537-11-5 | 2009 | $34.99 | Item: **920**

Phone: 1+ (360) 306-5369   **Fax:** (905) 481-0756   **Email:** info@enna.com

The Toyota Way in Sales and Marketing

Many companies today are trying to implement the ideas and principles of Lean into non-traditional environments, such as service centers, sales organizations and transactional environments. In this book Mr. Ishizaka provides insight on how to apply Lean operational principles and Kaizen to these dynamic and complicated environments.

ISBN 978-1-926537-08-5 | 2009 | $28.99 | Item: **918**

Training Packages

5S Training Package

Our 5S Solution Packages will help your company create a sustainable 5S program that will turn your shop floor around and put you ahead of the competition. All of the benefits that come from Lean Manufacturing are built upon a strong foundation of 5S. Enna's solution packages will show you how to implement and sustain an environment of continuous improvement.

Version 1: Sort, Straighten, Sweep, Standardize and Sustain
ISBN 978-0-973750-90-4 | 2005 | $429.99 | Item: **12**
Version 2: Sort, Set In Order, Shine, Standardize and Sustain
ISBN 978-1-897363-25-6 | 2006 | $429.99 | Item: **17**

Study Mission to Japan

We are excited to present an exclusive trip to the birthplace of Lean. We provide a one-week unique tour at a reasonable all-inclusive price that will guide you to a better understanding of Lean Manufacturing principles. Enna has exclusive access to Toyota and Toyota suppliers due to our publications of Dr. Shigeo Shingo's classic manuscripts. You will have one-on-one access to Japanese Lean Executives and learn from their experiences and solutions. We also offer custom private tours for executive management teams over 12 people. Join us on our next tour by visiting www.enna.com/japantrip and register on-line or by telephone at: +1 (360) 306-5369

To Order:
Mail orders and checks to:
Enna Products Corporation
ATTN: Order Processing
1602 Carolina Street, Unit B3
Bellingham, WA 98229, USA
Phone: +1 (360) 306-5369 • Fax: (905) 481-0756
Email: info@enna.com

We accept checks and all major credit cards.
Notice: All prices are in US Dollars and are subject to change without notice.

To Order: Enna Corp., 1602 Carolina Street, Unit B3, Bellingham, WA 98229

LaVergne, TN USA
15 November 2009
164150LV00003B/6/P

9 781897 363959